N O R F O L K
C O U N T R Y
H O U S E S
FROM THE AIR

NORFOLK COUNTRY HOUSES
FROM THE AIR

DEREK EDWARDS & TOM WILLIAMSON

Sutton Publishing

First published in 2000 by
Sutton Publishing Limited · Phoenix Mill
Thrupp · Stroud · Gloucestershire · GL5 2BU

British Library Cataloguing in Publication Data
A catalogue record for this book is available from the British Library

ISBN 0 7509 2347 4

Half-title page: East Barsham Manor, see p. 13.
Frontispiece: Dry conditions reveal a complex pattern of parchmarks in the gardens at Blickling Hall – traces of the elaborate parterres laid out by Lady Lothian in the late nineteenth century.

Typeset in 10/12 pt Sabon.
Typesetting and origination by
Sutton Publishing Limited.
Printed in Great Britain by
Bath Press Ltd, Bath.

CONTENTS

ACKNOWLEDGEMENTS

Many Norfolk people have provided help and contributed information for this book, especially members of Norfolk Landscape Archaeology and staff and students of the Centre of East Anglian Studies at the University of East Anglia. Particular thanks go to Linda Campbell, David Cubitt, Brian Cushion, Jon Dye, Jon Finch, Emma Hazell, Rob Liddiard, Alan Mackley, Beverley Peters, Ivan Ringwood, A. Hassell Smith, Anthea Taigel, Susanna Wade Martins, Fin Pickard, Susie West, Richard Wilson, and Nigel Wright. Thanks also to Phillip Judge, who supplied all the line drawings except 89, which is by Alan Mackley. Many thanks to the Royal Institute of British Architects, for permission to reproduce 106; the staff of the Norfolk Record Office, for permission to reproduce 13 and for all their usual help and advice; the Norfolk Museums' Service, for permission to reproduce 35 and 58; Lord Leicester, for permission to reproduce 69; Lord Walpole, for permission to reproduce 99; Mr Prideaux-Brune and English Heritage, for permission to reproduce 39, 47 and 53; and to all the landowners who kindly allowed access to their properties and archives.

1. Weasenham Hall, Weasenham All Saints. This large neo-Jacobean house was erected as late as 1905 by the 2nd Earl of Leicester as a home for his second wife and children. It is now in a poor state of repair and, at the time of going to press, the Coke family were seeking to have it demolished.

INTRODUCTION

This book examines the large houses built by major landowners in Norfolk from the fifteenth to the end of the nineteenth century, and the ornamental landscapes that were laid out around them. Although the great age of country house building came to an end with the onset of agricultural depression in the 1880s, large mansions and their parks and gardens make an immense impact on the county's landscape even today. Some have been demolished, but many still survive: and even where they do not, their parks, lodges and other features often remain, signalling their former presence.

A country house generally stood at the centre of a large landed estate, a part of which was retained 'in hand' as a home farm, while the rest was leased out to tenant farmers. Their rents paid for the creation and maintenance of the mansion and its grounds – although many landed families also possessed alternative sources of income in the form of investments, the proceeds of government office or rental income from property in other counties. Not all the owners of the country houses discussed in this volume were equally wealthy. At one extreme were the largest landowners – families like the Townshends of Raynham, or the Walpoles of Houghton, whose estates extended over 10,000 acres or more (in the most extreme case, that of the Coke's Holkham estate, across more than 43,000 acres). Such people were frequently prominent in local and national politics: they might serve as courtiers, MPs, even (in the case of Sir Robert Walpole) as Prime Minister. Below this group – which never consisted of more than a dozen or so families in the county – was a far more numerous company: the local gentry, those landowners with estates embracing, at most, two or three parishes. The lower ranks of this group might own no more than a few hundred acres and have a lifestyle little different from that of the farmers below them.

The composition of these two broad groups of landowners did not remain stable and unchanging over the long period covered by this book. Many minor landed families disappeared altogether in the course of time; so too, especially in the later seventeenth and early eighteenth centuries, did some of the major ones, particularly those who – like the Pastons of Oxnead – had backed the wrong side in the Civil War. There was also a steady stream of new recruits to the landed classes. In the seventeenth and eighteenth centuries, these were often people who had made their fortune in government service and the law: men like Cyril Wynch, a politician who amassed a fortune in Ireland, spent £12,000 buying up property around Methwold, and died in 1707 worth, it was said, £100,000. In the nineteenth century, in contrast, such men were more likely to have made their money in finance or trade. In all periods, however, upwardly mobile families from outside the ranks of the landed rich had one principal aim: to join them. Everyone's ideal was to own a house in the country, set within extensive grounds and with a landed estate attached.

Nevertheless, while there was a high degree of social mobility, there was also a marked degree of stability, at least in the period from the middle of the seventeenth century until the end of the nineteenth. The Walpoles of Houghton, the Cokes of Holkham, the Townshends of Raynham, the Astleys of Melton Constable, the Wodehouses of Kimberley, the de Greys of Merton, the Windhams of Felbrigg had all been important families at the time of the Restoration, and were still among the leading landowners in the county in 1873, when the New Domesday allows us to see, for the first time since 1086, the distribution of landed wealth in Norfolk.

The holdings of the greatest landowners were not distributed evenly throughout the county. By the early eighteenth century, and probably for some time before, the largest

2. The site of Warham Hall and its gardens, revealed as a pattern of soil marks. The hall was demolished at the start of the nineteenth century following the acquisition of the Warham estate by Thomas William Coke of Holkham. The layout of paths within the gardens, and even the site of a central pond, are all clearly visible. The position of the house forms a more confused pattern of marks towards the top of the picture.

estates clustered on the lighter and more acid soils in the north and west of the county: areas devoted to cereal cultivation and sheep farming, in which small landowners found it hard to make much of a living during times of recession and where land was comparatively cheap. Where the soil was more fertile (and more expensive), and where cattle-farming and dairying played a more important role in the agrarian economy, large estates were much less prominent, although the local gentry were often well represented. The claylands in the south of the county, the Fens to the west, the fertile loams of Flegg and the Broadland marshes were all areas like this.

There are many approaches to the investigation of country houses and their grounds. This volume is written from both historical and archaeological perspectives. By studying the plan of a building or the disposition of features within a landscape we can often learn something of the unspoken or unconscious attitudes and assumptions ordering the patterns of everyday life. Great houses and their landscapes embody the aspirations and beliefs of the rulers of rural society, and changes in their design express changes in these attitudes. And it is from the air that the spatial organisation of a house and its grounds are most easily appreciated: the relationship of a mansion to the kitchen garden, to stables and offices, to park and garden, and to other dwellings in the locality. It is from the air, too, that traces of long-vanished houses and gardens are most clearly revealed, as networks of parch or soil marks, or as low banks and scarps in the turf (1). In the pages that follow we will combine aerial photographs with maps, plans and illustrations to display Norfolk's rich legacy of country houses in new and revealing ways.

1
TUDOR AND STUART
COUNTRY HOUSES

Tudor and Stuart country houses developed out of the defended residences of late medieval times, but these were already more than simple fortifications, refuges against wars and violence. The moats around large manor houses such as Elsing (3) or Mannington (4) were as much for display as for serious defence: they would never have done more than deter casual intruders. Even the 'castles' of the fifteenth century, although they had a more serious defensive purpose, were also designed for comfortable living. Caister Castle, built for Sir John Fastolfe in the 1430s and '40s, is one of the most impressive examples in England, with its regular rectangular plan, corner towers, gun ports, and the great, soaring main tower, more than 27 metres high (6). An impressive structure, certainly, but one in which the needs of defence were beginning to give way to the demands of comfort. The large window near the base of the tower would have been an inviting target for any attacker.

3. Elsing Hall was originally built in the 1460s, although extensively restored in the nineteenth century.

4. Mannington Hall is broadly contemporary with Elsing – a licence to crenellate was granted in 1451 and the building was under construction in 1460. Here, too, the building was extensively restored in the nineteenth century, in this case by the 2nd Earl of Orford.

Little of the main gatehouse at Caister has survived but it was clearly a massive structure. This was the norm: in the last centuries of the Middle Ages it was the gatehouse that was usually the most imposing feature of a castle. Baconsthorpe, built between 1450 and 1486 by the Heydon family, is Norfolk's only other well-preserved late medieval castle. Like Caister, it occupies a moated site and has a fairly regular, rectangular plan. The low walls and several towers still survive, but it is the massive gatehouse that dominates the scene, especially when viewed from the air (7).

THE COURTYARD TRADITION

Caister and Baconsthorpe were among the last buildings constructed in Norfolk that could seriously be described as 'castles'. At the end of the fifteenth century the county's leading families were still erecting moated houses – and some were provided with battlements, towers and imposing gatehouses – but these were not primarily defensive buildings. Middleton Towers, near King's Lynn, was constructed in the 1460s. Only the great brick gatehouse with its four corner turrets has survived (the other buildings within the moat are of Victorian date) (8). This structure was clearly capable of withstanding a limited assault, but once again the fine oriel window, projecting out above the bridge, clearly indicates that defence was not the prime consideration of its builder, Thomas, 7th Lord Scales. A better preserved example of the same kind of building – indeed, one of the most imposing late medieval residences in England – is Oxburgh Hall, built in the 1480s by Sir Edmund Bedingfeld and now owned by the National Trust (9). Built of brick, its moated site, crenellated parapets and arrow-slits express military pretensions and would indeed have served to ward off a limited attack. Particularly prominent, from the air as much as from the ground, is the soaring gatehouse, with its polygonal turrets rising to a height of seven storeys. This is even provided with *machicolations*, openings through which stones and other missiles could be hurled at anyone trying to force an entry into the courtyard. These, however, were ornamental rather than functional: nothing could be dropped through them for they were sealed with stone. The wide windows in the gatehouse and

5. The site of Buxton Manor. One of many examples of abandoned moated residences in Norfolk. Here the moat has been filled in, but its shape, and the outlines of some of the buildings that stood within it, are revealed from the air as a pattern of cropmarks.

6. Sir John Fastolfe began building Caister Castle in 1432. The castle is dominated by the soaring drum tower, five storeys and 27 metres high. An inventory of 1459 lists no fewer than three halls and twenty-six chambers, as well as service rooms, but their precise layout is unknown. The castle was ranged around two main courts; the layout of the west range of the Upper Court is marked out approximately in concrete.

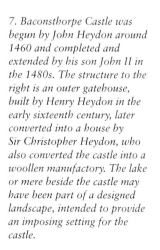

7. Baconsthorpe Castle was begun by John Heydon around 1460 and completed and extended by his son John II in the 1480s. The structure to the right is an outer gatehouse, built by Henry Heydon in the early sixteenth century, later converted into a house by Sir Christopher Heydon, who also converted the castle into a woollen manufactory. The lake or mere beside the castle may have been part of a designed landscape, intended to provide an imposing setting for the castle.

8. Middleton Towers is slightly earlier than Oxburgh (see picture 9); so far as the evidence goes, it seems it was begun by the 7th Lord Scales, who was killed by a Yorkist mob in London in 1459. Scales's work was continued by Anthony Woodville, who married Scales's daughter in 1460, but the building was never completed: Woodville, now the 2nd Earl Rivers, was murdered at Pontefract by Richard III. By the end of the eighteenth century the building was derelict and the moat largely filled in, but in 1856 the site was purchased by Sir Lewis Whincop Jarvis, who restored the gatehouse and completely rebuilt the remains of the adjacent west wing. The corner tower was erected in the 1870s and the wing running north from this was added at the end of the century by the Ramsden family.

9. Oxburgh Hall, the finest late medieval house in Norfolk, was built in the 1480s by Sir Edmund Bedingfeld. Typically, it was ranged around four sides of a courtyard, surrounded by a moat, and entered through an imposing gatehouse. The south or hall range, opposite the gatehouse, was demolished in 1778 but was rebuilt, and the rest of the building extensively restored, by Sir Henry Bedingfeld in the middle decades of the nineteenth century. The project signalled the restoration of the family fortunes through Sir Henry's judicious marriage to the wealthy heiress Margaret Paston. The house is now owned by the National Trust.

elsewhere were for comfort and easy living, not for defence. The architecture was supposed to inspire awe, and evoke memories of a chivalric age: to be seriously defensible the building would have required gun-ports, not arrow-slits.

This building probably owes its survival to the fact that in later times the fortunes of the Bedingfelds were rather mixed. The family were Catholics, and supporters of the Royalist cause in the Civil War. These allegiances brought a variety of economic penalties and disadvantages, and thus prevented a thorough rebuilding of the antiquated residence in the seventeenth or eighteenth centuries. The hall was, nevertheless, added to and modified over the years. The most dramatic change came in 1778, when the southern hall range was demolished (it was rebuilt in the nineteenth century). It is, however, possible to reconstruct the arrangement of the original building by using a plan made in the previous year (10). The layout was typical of great houses of the period. The building was not only moated, but ranged around four sides of a central courtyard. Visitors would have crossed the drawbridge and passed through the gatehouse into the courtyard. Immediately ahead they would have seen the hall range, entered through a porch – an imposing affair, as was appropriate to the most important part of the residence. Moving inside, visitors would have found themselves within the 'screens passage', a corridor leading transversely across the width of the building. To one side was the great hall, nearly 12 metres long, 6 metres wide and some 6 metres high, with a magnificent timber roof and a great oriel window. This was the principal public room of the house, used for a wide variety of everyday business, as well as for great set-piece occasions such as feasts. On the other side of the corridor were the service rooms, the buttery and pantry, for the storage and preparation of food. The private rooms of the owner and his family were located beyond the far end of the hall, the 'upper end'. Here on the ground floor was the parlour, a kind of general bed-sitting room. Above was the great chamber, in which the family would normally have dined.

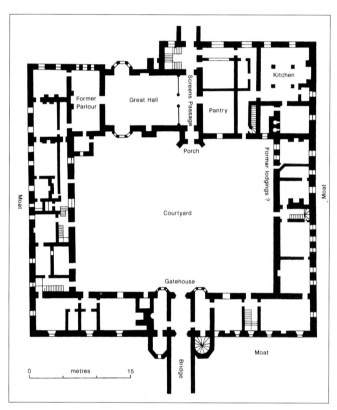

10. The original layout of Oxburgh Hall, based on a plan made shortly before the demolition of the hall range in 1778.

The contents of the other ranges at Oxburgh are less clear – by the eighteenth century they contained a diverse collection of service and reception rooms – but it is probable that the western range was occupied by storerooms and the other domestic facilities necessary to sustain the household, while the eastern comprised 'lodgings' or apartments for retainers and guests, each separately accessed from the courtyard. For great families like the Bedingfelds did not, like their descendants in later centuries, live alone in their houses, accompanied only by menial servants. Instead, their households included a number of officers and officials, normally drawn from local gentry families, who helped in the administration of the great house and the estate. Most establishments of any size also included a chaplain and a tutor, as well as a number of trained fighters who could, when required, offer some protection to the lord and his family – a necessary insurance in a turbulent age. The gatehouse at Oxburgh provided a particularly magnificent set of lodgings that could be used to accommodate prestigious visitors: the main rooms within it are still called the King's Room and the Queen's Room, after Henry VII and his wife Elizabeth of York who came here – together with the Earls of Devonshire, Essex, Northumberland, Oxford, and Suffolk and their retinues – in 1487.

Not all courtyard houses were built at a stroke like Oxburgh. Some, including Hunstanton, developed their form gradually, as range was added to range in a piecemeal fashion (11). Here the oldest surviving section is the gatehouse, erected around 1490 by Sir Roger le Strange (whose family had held the manor since the twelfth century). The gatehouse was built shortly after his appointment in 1486 as High Sheriff of the county and, as at Oxburgh, it was intended more for show than for serious defence: Roger's arms and those of his wife are proudly displayed in the spandrels of the arch. This imposing structure must have been accompanied by a hall range on the opposite side of the moated island, but this does not survive. It was demolished and rebuilt in 1578 as a large 'double pile' building – i.e., one that was two rooms deep. A map of 1615 shows the double-gable roof and the central chimneys of this impressive edifice. There were further alterations in the 1620s, when Sir Hamon le Strange added a forecourt on the outside of the moat, complete with an elaborate Renaissance gateway, visible to the right on picture 11. More importantly, he constructed two 'T'-shaped side wings, which linked the gatehouse to the hall range and thus created a courtyard plan. A fire of 1853 gutted the hall range. This was followed by drastic rebuilding and then by another fire in the 1940s, but it is still possible to see the impressive entrance porch added by le Strange in 1618: a fashionable Renaissance feature with two columns carrying obelisks, set in front of a rather elegant background of diapered (patterned) brickwork.

Several other great courtyard houses, similar in scale and layout to Oxburgh or Hunstanton, have largely or entirely disappeared from the Norfolk landscape. One example is Hales Hall, built by Sir James Hobart, attorney-general to Henry VII (12).

11. Hunstanton Hall is another late medieval house built of brick within a substantial moat. The gatehouse was erected by Sir Roger le Strange around 1490 but the flanking ranges are seventeenth century. The great hall to the east was lost in a fire in 1853 and replaced by a Victorian building. To the east (right) an outer courtyard is entered through an elaborate Renaissance gateway, added by Sir Hamon le Strange in the early seventeenth century.

12. *Hales Hall: the site of the mansion erected by Sir James Hobart, Attorney-General to Henry VII. Only the barns and service ranges of an outer courtyard survive.*

13. *Shelton Hall, one of several late medieval mansions in Norfolk which have disappeared from the landscape. The hall, reminiscent of Oxburgh, was erected in the late fifteenth century by Sir Ralph Shelton. Only the moat, and a few fragments of masonry, now survive, but the building is clearly shown in this undated seventeenth-century drawing.*

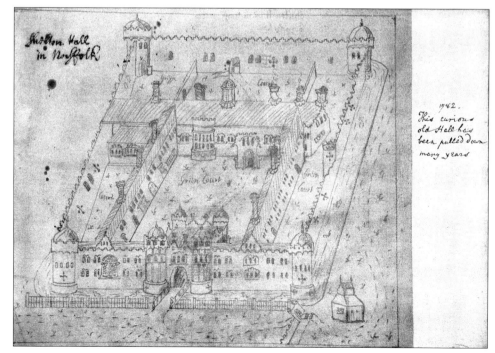

Here only the substantial north and south ranges and the gateway still remain. The principal hall block has disappeared. Another example is Shelton Hall in the claylands of south Norfolk, built in the late fifteenth century by Sir Ralph Shelton. Extensive remains of this building still survived in the eighteenth century, when the historian Blomefield described the

> Grand antique mansion or MANOR-house, built by Sir Ralph Shelton, in a square form, with an outside wall imbattled, and a turret at each corner, moated in, with a grand gate space at the entrance, and a turret at each corner of it. In the windows and ceilings were many coats of the matches of the Sheltons, &c., but the whole is now ruinated.

Only very minor traces now remain, but the mansion is illustrated in a small drawing, probably of the mid-seventeenth century (13). The remains of Wodehouses' Tower – the great residence of the Wodehouse family at Kimberley – suggest that this, too, was ranged around four sides of a courtyard, entered by imposing gatehouses, and surrounded by a moat (14). Kenninghall Palace – the great residence of the Dukes of Norfolk, built in the 1520s and '30s – was also apparently ranged around two courtyards, although its site was not moated. Only a fragment of this substantial house survives as a farmhouse and its original form remains unclear.

There were a number of reasons why most large residences were built to this kind of plan. One was that even the greatest houses of the period were generally of 'single-

14. The site of Wodehouses' Tower, in the park of Kimberley Hall, the great moated house erected by Sir John Wodehouse in the fifteenth century. Queen Elizabeth was entertained here in August 1578. The earthworks outside the moat are of varied origins. Some represent field boundaries, access roads and associated buildings, but some may be the remains of medieval or Tudor gardens.

pile' construction – that is, they were only one room deep (the hall range at Hunstanton was a rare exception to this rule). In part this was because of structural demands – it was much easier and cheaper to provide a roof for a comparatively thin building. But it was partly a hangover from an earlier period, when window glass had been in short supply and windows had been provided with wooden shutters, ensuring that – unless a room had windows on two sides – shutting out the wind and rain on one side might plunge its occupants into darkness. A small single-pile house, like the farmhouses erected in large numbers in sixteenth- and seventeenth-century Norfolk, could easily take the form of a simple rectangle. But the greatest landowners required more extensive accommodation. Rather than simply add room to room in a long, attenuated sequence, a more visually appealing and convenient arrangement was to turn the corner, creating blocks at right angles to the main range. In the largest houses the building was further extended around the fourth side, thus producing the by now familiar enclosed, quadrangular plan with central courtyard. Such a compact layout was also, of course, dictated by the fact that many of these houses were built within constricted moated enclosures. And while, as we have said, defence was not the primary consideration of the builders, security was of some concern. A courtyard plan, entered through a single gateway, allowed the comings and goings of visitors to be monitored by a porter positioned in a lodge – a practice still perpetuated in the colleges of Oxford and Cambridge.

As the early development of Hunstanton shows, not all great houses in this period were ranged around all four sides of a courtyard. Some, especially in the sixteenth century, occupied only three sides: that is, they remained open on the entrance side, giving the house a plan like a half 'H' or – because of the frequent addition of a substantial central porch to the hall range – an 'E'. Such houses still usually had a splendid gatehouse, for this was *de rigueur* among the rich in the fifteenth and sixteenth centuries. But it was linked to the side wings by walls rather than by ranges of buildings. Such truncated plans were not necessarily the consequence of an owner's poverty. Some contemporaries urged that one side of the courtyard should be left open because the somewhat enclosed and claustrophobic character of the traditional plan was unhealthy. Indeed, some of the most powerful families in Norfolk built houses like this. The Pastons' great mansion at Oxnead, for example, was ranged around only three sides of a courtyard (due to the subsequent decline in the fortunes of the family only one wing of this huge mansion survives). Channonz Hall in Tibbenham, the home of the powerful Buxton family, was similar in appearance and experienced a similar

15. *Channonz Hall, Tibbenham, shown as a detail on a fine map of 1640. The great mansion of the Buxton family was ranged around only three sides of a courtyard, with a free-standing gatehouse occupying much of the fourth side.*

fate. Here, however, the original layout is known from a fine map of *c.* 1640 (15). The red-brick mansion, probably erected in the 1560s or '70s, had an 'E'-shaped plan and walls that ran forward to enclose the courtyard. They met at an imposing gatehouse with turrets and battlements. This did not actually stand on the edge of the moat, however, and by 1640 there was a wide outer forecourt in front of it, apparently entered through a smaller, ornamental gateway, an arrangement reminiscent of that at Hunstanton.

Numerous smaller manor houses were built in Norfolk in the sixteenth and early seventeenth centuries by less prestigious families – that is, by members of the local gentry – who were benefiting from a general expansion in the agricultural economy, stimulated by rising population. Where enough money was available, such people generally adopted a version of the fashionable 'E'-shaped plan, the centre of the hall

range provided with a porch which, particularly in the sixteenth century, might be imposing, like that at Fincham Hall, which is almost a small tower. Sometimes the fourth side of the courtyard was provided with a gatehouse, as at Denver Hall, built in the 1570s. Quite how common such an arrangement was remains unclear, however, because of later wholesale demolitions. At Barnham Broom Hall, for example, a gatehouse complete with drawbridge survived as late as 1849 but was then demolished and has left no trace. Such features were probably only found among more prosperous members of the gentry. This was a very diverse social group and while its richest members might share something of the lifestyle of the greatest landowners, its lower strata merged almost imperceptibly with the class of yeomen farmer below. The poorer gentry consequently had houses little different from large farmhouses, rectangular blocks containing a simple sequence of service rooms/hall/parlour, although they often had a fine porch, on which they might display the coats of arms that proclaimed their ancestral status.

From late medieval times large houses in Norfolk were, like those of other parts of southern and eastern England, increasingly built of brick. Oxburgh was one of the earliest to be entirely constructed of this material, but it was soon widely adopted. The high-status nature of the new medium encouraged its flamboyant use in elaborate chimneys, mouldings, and angle pilasters. Perhaps the most striking sixteenth-century house in the county is East Barsham Manor, built by Sir Henry Fermor in the reign of Henry VIII, although it was much restored and extended in the nineteenth century (16). This has a riot of decorative brickwork, with tall octagonal pilasters along the walls and, in particular, at the corners; decorative chimneys; and brick friezes.

16. East Barsham Manor was erected in the 1520s by Sir Henry Fermor. It was heavily restored in the nineteenth century. A riot of ornamental brickwork, it is entered by a tall brick gatehouse in the medieval manner and boasts turrets and crenellations; but these are pure embellishment – the building was never intended even to look really defendable.

THE IMPACT OF THE RENAISSANCE

17. Blickling Hall, built between 1619 and 1626 for Sir Henry Hobart, James I's Lord Chief Justice, and designed by the architect Robert Lyminge. The symmetrical façade is made more impressive by the frame of the great entrance court, flanked by long service ranges. Although at the cutting edge of fashion, the house was built on an earlier moated site and ranged around two courtyards, the larger – to the north – being open on its north side. Hobart also retained part of the earlier medieval building that had stood on this moated site – the west range – but this was rebuilt in the 1760s and '70s by the Ivory brothers. At the same time the north side was filled with a new range. Both ranges were in the same style as the original building, an unusual choice for the period.

East Barsham, like Oxburgh and Hunstanton, is decorated with crenellations which, with its large gatehouse, give the house something of the air of a castle. But in the more peaceful climate of the Tudor regime such signs of martial display gradually declined in popularity. Moreover, as the influence of Renaissance ideas from Italy began to be felt, more emphasis was placed not only on making the elevations of a mansion's main ranges symmetrical, but also on using classical forms – pillars, pediments – for windows and doors. This was not simply a matter of 'fashion'. It reflected new systems of values among the upper echelons of society.

With the accession of the Tudors and the development of a more peaceful society, rivalries between different families within the county were now played out through the medium of the courtroom, or through intrigues at the royal court. As a result, real or imagined ability as a warrior became less important as a sign of status, and more emphasis was given to the acquisition of the kind of social skills necessary for promotion at court: knowledge of classical and Renaissance civilisation, and of art and literature; an ability to dance or play music, and to hold a witty and amusing conversation. The leaders of county society moulded their houses accordingly and their social inferiors among the local gentry gradually followed suit. Thus the interior decoration of Blickling Hall, Sir Henry Hobart's great house built between 1619 and 1626, is full of puns and allusions that only the educated could understand. The most remarkable room is the Long Gallery, an example of a new kind of living area that developed in Tudor England. A long, imposing space suitable for a variety of indoor pastimes, its ceiling is decorated with complex plasterwork featuring a

number of *emblems* – designs derived from classical or biblical mythology, intended to 'feede at once both the minde and eie'. Such objects of contemplation were designed, therefore, to improve the mind and character. Like much of the other decoration in the house, they also served by implication to identify Blickling's owner, a man who had grown rich in the law and government service, as a person of education and knowledge, able to understand the allusions and thus, almost by definition, fit to be a member of the elite. In common with others from a similar background, however, Hobart also used symbols of martial valour in the decoration and ornament of the house, including the bearded, sword-carrying warriors carved on the newel posts of the staircase.

Blickling is a magnificent house: its 'architect and builder', according to the entry in the Blickling parish register recording his death, was Robert Lyminge (17). Seven years earlier he had finished supervising the construction of one of the greatest houses in Tudor England, Hatfield House in Hertfordshire, for Robert Cecil, Earl of Salisbury. There are obvious similarities between the two buildings: both have prominent corner turrets topped by leaded domes; both have shaped gables on the main façade, punctuating the roof line; and both have an entrance decorated with classical pillars, although the one at Blickling is rather less magnificent than that at Hatfield. Blickling is now owned by the National Trust.

In some ways the house's plan was innovative, in some ways backward-looking. It had a long gallery and a number of private rooms – to the great chamber had now been

18. Heydon Hall. The main range of this fine building was built by Henry Dynne, one of the Auditors of the Exchequer, in the 1580s: unusually, the house was two rooms deep and in spite of its size and wealth it was not ranged around a courtyard or approached through a gatehouse.

19. Barningham Hall was built some thirty years later than Heydon – the porch carries a date of 1612 – for Sir Edward Paston. An imposing building, with its two-storeyed dormer windows and tall porch, it was altered and extended by John Adey Repton and Humphry Repton between 1805 and 1807.

added a withdrawing chamber and bedchamber, wrapped around the front of the building at first-floor level. But it occupied an earlier moated site, was ranged around two small courtyards, and the main entrance still originally gave access to a screens passage across the lower end of the hall. The main façade, however, was framed by an imposing entrance court, flanked by service ranges providing a most impressive approach.

Blickling was not the only house to be built around a courtyard at such a late date. The gatehouse at Merton Hall, for example, was erected in c. 1620. But as Renaissance ideas became better understood, and as the demands for internal as well as external symmetry became more pressing, the days of the traditional plan were numbered. Moreover, large landowners in this period had less desire than formerly to maintain large households, and this reduced the need for the ranges of lodgings that had been such a feature of houses like Oxburgh. The inward-looking nature of courtyard houses must also have seemed increasingly anachronistic, and from the later sixteenth century some substantial buildings began to be erected, which, so far as the evidence of the surviving structures indicates, were always compact, without side wings, courtyards or gatehouses. Close attention was now paid to external symmetry, with the house entered through a central porch. Examples include Heydon Hall, built in the 1580s for Henry Dynne, one of the Auditors of the Exchequer (18); Felbrigg Hall, built c. 1610 for Thomas Windham; and Barningham, erected in 1612 for Sir Edward Paston (19). Heydon was a particularly innovative house in that it was a double-pile structure, two rooms deep. But the house that most decisively rejected older practices was Raynham Hall, where construction began in 1619. This was unquestionably the most original and advanced house to be built in Norfolk in

20. *Raynham Hall, begun in 1621, was an innovative building, designed by its owner, Sir Roger Townshend and his 'mason' William Edge. A substantial triple-pile structure, with Dutch gables and precise classical windows, the house shows the influence of the new Palladian ideas of the fashionable architect Inigo Jones. The building was, however, much altered – probably under William Kent's direction – in the 1730s. In the foreground, earthworks and parchmarks pick out the outlines of the seventeenth-century gardens.*

the period before the Civil War (20). It was apparently designed by its owner Sir Roger Townshend in association with the 'mason', William Edge. Its form and layout were influenced by a number of contemporary experiments in architecture, such as the Prince's Lodgings at Newmarket, designed by the great architect Inigo Jones, and possibly also by Continental models, for Townshend and Edge seem to have travelled together to the Low Countries shortly before and during the building's construction.

Building work seems to have continued almost up until the outbreak of the Civil War in 1642. Raynham is a compact structure, two rooms deep and largely symmetrical in internal layout as well as in external elevation. Its façades are dominated by 'Dutch' gables – shaped gables with pediments – and its windows and doors are carefully proportioned vertical rectangles with pediments. It was, and is, an imposing structure. Townshend, like other innovative designers of the seventeenth century, was unable to reject all aspects of the traditional plan and in particular had problems with the layout and position of the main entrance in relation to the hall. He clearly felt that the main door ought to give access to a cross-passage at one end of the hall: but such an arrangement was difficult to reconcile with a high degree of internal symmetry. Thus it was that, instead of entering the hall directly, the front entrance led into a kind of residual screens passage that ran around each end of it (21) – a curious compromise of old and new. (This arrangement no longer survives: it was modified, together with other aspects of the building, in the following century.)

21. The original layout of the ground floor at Raynham Hall, as shown on a drawing of 1671. The plan is highly symmetrical but the two entrances still lead into screens passages, running along both ends of the hall.

TUDOR AND STUART GARDENS

We know comparatively little about the gardens laid out around late medieval residences in Norfolk. Recent archaeological research suggests that some castles may have had elaborate landscaped settings, making use in particular of large areas of water: the

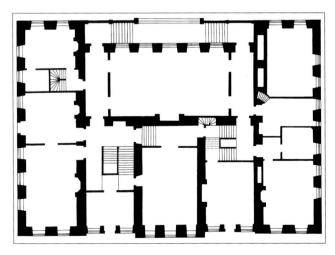

wide, lake-like moat at Bodiam in Sussex and the extensive 'mere' beside Kenilworth Castle in Warwickshire are good examples. In a similar way, the great lake or mere beside the castle at Baconsthorpe was probably not simply a large fish-pond but part of a grand landscaping scheme, designed to set the castle off to great effect (7). Some of the earthworks around the Wodehouses' great mansion at Kimberley (14) may likewise represent the remains of some kind of water garden, and associated areas of garden and orchard, although what survives has not been closely dated.

The same is true of the earthworks at Oxburgh. A map of *c.* 1722 shows that the land to the east of the house was occupied by kitchen gardens and parterres, while to the south, in the low-lying area between the moat and the river, lay an area described as 'The Quarters', and beyond the river another labelled 'The Walks'. Few details are shown of what lay within either compartment, but aerial photography and archaeological survey have provided further information (22 and 23). The Quarters contains a curious arrangement of raised banks, perhaps the remains of a garden broadly contemporary with the house. The more diffuse pattern of low, amorphous, parallel banks to the south of this represents the line of the old river, diverted to its present course some time in the eighteenth century.

We know more about the gardens laid out around Tudor and Stuart country houses in Norfolk. Such evidence as there is suggests that they were characterised – as elsewhere in England – by highly geometric designs. Their principal features were 'knots' and 'parterres' (that is, horizontal patterns defined by planting, gravel or turf) and topiary (shrubs cut into abstract geometric shapes). To our eyes such gardens would appear highly artificial and probably rather garish. At Stiffkey in the 1590s the lower terrace of the gardens was laid out as beds edged with two or three courses of brickwork topped with posts and rails painted black and white heraldic colours of the owners, the Bacon family. The centrepiece was a knot planted with thyme and hyssop, and the surrounding ground was covered in clay stained white and black to match the posts.

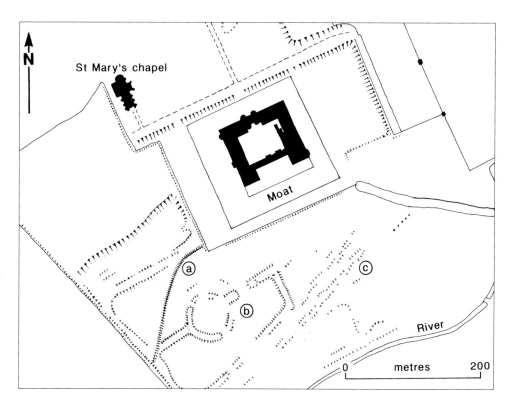

22. Earthworks in the parkland to the south and west of Oxburgh. The bank 'a' marks the line of an outflow pipe from the moat; the confused banks and scarps at 'c' represent the line of the stream, altered in the eighteenth century. The curious earthworks at 'b' evidently relate to some kind of garden, possibly late medieval, possibly of Tudor date.

In most cases, these gardens were surrounded by high walls that served to separate clearly their formal structure from the less ordered environment around them. They also provided a sheltered microclimate for flowers and fruit trees (the collection of numerous different varieties of fruit trees, and to a lesser extent other types of plant, was something of an obsession among the gentry), and also for the owner, his family and guests as they enjoyed the garden. Such advantages were, perhaps, especially important in an area like Norfolk, noted for its late springs. In addition, walls were a logical way of enclosing a garden around a residence that was itself ranged around a courtyard, and provided another opportunity for the excessive and self-conscious display of the new material: brick. They were generally crenellated and provided with elaborate gateways – like those that still survive at Besthorpe Hall (25).

The garden was usually only one of a network of enclosures surrounding a manor house. The others contained farmyards, stable-yards, fish-ponds, orchards and nut grounds, and all the other facilities necessary to sustain the household. These enclosures and the gardens themselves were often arranged in a somewhat chaotic fashion. In part this was probably because they tended to develop piecemeal, with owners adding and subtracting elements as taste dictated or need demanded: the few surviving examples of early walled gardens in the county – most notably those at Besthorpe, Intwood, and Kirby Cane – incorporate a number of different phases. At Intwood, for example, the surviving pre-nineteenth-century enclosures are defined by walls of sixteenth-, early seventeenth- and mid-seventeenth-century date (24). Walls were not the only 'hard landscaping' found within these gardens. Many also

24. *Intwood Hall. The hall in its present form appears late nineteenth century but the Victorian gothic brickwork is a veneer encasing a Neoclassical house built at the start of the century, which itself incorporates fragments of the house erected by Sir Richard Gresham in the mid-sixteenth century. The walled gardens that survive to the north of the hall are similarly of varied dates, with walls of sixteenth-, seventeenth-, eighteenth- and nineteenth-century construction.*

25. *A late sixteenth-century garden gate at Besthorpe Hall, near Attleborough.*

contained summer houses and 'banqueting houses', buildings in which a final course to a meal would be taken, the owner and guests retiring here from the more formal surroundings of the hall or great chamber. Good examples of such structures survive at Bawburgh and Kirby Cane.

A map of 1654, showing Brooke Hall in the south of the county, reveals a typical range of features: enclosed courts, one (presumably a garden) with an elaborate gateway; barns and other farm buildings; a complex of fish-ponds; and areas of orchard and coppice (26). The presence of fish-ponds close to the mansion was particularly common. The purpose of these 'stews' or holding ponds was, in the words of Roger North of Rougham:

To maintain Fish for the daily Use of your House and Friends, whereby you may with little Trouble, and at any Time, take out all or any Fish they contain: therefore it is good to place them in some inclos'd Ground near the chief Mansion House. Some Recess in a Garden is very proper, because the Fish are fenc'd from Robbers, and your Journey to them is Short and easy, and your Eye will be often upon them, which will conduce to their being well kept, and they will be an Ornament to the Walks.

Dovecotes were also often located close to the house and proudly displayed, partly because they were a potent symbol of status. They were by law a prerogative of the manorial gentry, the 'right onely & badge of a lordship or signorye', according to Hamon le Strange of Hunstanton Hall. The dovecote also produced something else of particular importance in the domestic economy: 'Dovesdunge is an excellent compost & Mucke for enriching of Grounds', as le Strange observed, and dovecotes were often positioned close to the main garden areas.

There were important differences between the gardens of the greater landowners and those of the local gentry. Individuals in the former group were generally involved in national politics, travelled extensively and were less directly involved in estate administration. They were usually more aware of national and international fashions, and their gardens often displayed a confident familiarity with Renaissance ideas, as expressed in the design of great villas and their grounds in contemporary Italy. In particular, the landed elite arranged their garden courts with more care than most local squires, and showed a greater interest in combining the design of the house and garden in a single scheme, sometimes embodying sophisticated mathematical principles. Moreover, their gardens were not always enclosed on all sides by high walls, but might in part be placed on open terraces so that views out across the surrounding landscape could be enjoyed. In some cases they contained such characteristically Italianate features as water gardens, grottoes and classical sculptures.

26. Detail from a map of Brooke, 1654, showing Brooke Hall surrounded by service buildings, orchards, gardens and fish-ponds.

Stiffkey, on the north coast of the county, is one example. The hall and its surroundings were designed by Sir Nicholas Bacon (Lord Keeper under Elizabeth I) in the 1570s, but largely constructed by his son Nathaniel after his death in 1579. The hall – which is now partly ruined – is still bounded on the east by elaborate terraced gardens which provide fine views over the river valley to the south (27). To the north of the house a walled garden, with an internal terrace, still survives. But other garden areas and courts to the south and west of the hall, and a straight canal which originally bounded the site to the south, no longer exist. In true Renaissance fashion, hall and gardens were designed as a single unified scheme, embodying abstract geometric principles: letters from Sir Nicholas, requesting information about the dimensions of the site and of existing features (such as the churchyard) within and around it, still survive. It seems, however, that the original plan was compromised by the fact that it was executed by his son, on somewhat uneven terrain, and by local builders and craftsmen. Even so, it is noteworthy that the length of the garden court to the east of the house – about 225 feet – is twice that of the house itself (127 feet). Similarly, it is likely that originally the distance across the whole site from north to south was twice that across the width of the house. Similar use of ratios and proportions can be identified in the internal layout of the house itself. This, nevertheless, has a somewhat old-fashioned appearance, with its tall corner turrets and central courtyard, entered on the south through a fine Renaissance

27. *Stiffkey Hall, north Norfolk.*
The house and gardens were
designed together by Sir Nicholas
Bacon, Lord Keeper to Elizabeth I.
Construction began in 1576 but
Bacon died in 1579 and the work
was completed under the
direction of his son Nathaniel,
for whom the estate had been
purchased. The house – only part
of which survives – was ranged
around three sides of a
courtyard, entered by the ornate
gateway visible in front of the
main structure, now converted
into a barn. The gardens were
laid out on terraces, providing
views across the valley of the
River Stiffkey; the church formed
an element in this elaborately
designed landscape.

gateway, the remains of which are visible in the centre of 27. (This also shows clearly the relationship between hall and gardens, and the churchyard to the north-east, which was incorporated as an integral feature of the design.) The hall passed to Sir Roger Townshend, Nathaniel's grandson, following the latter's death in 1622. After the construction of Raynham Hall the site declined to the status of a farmhouse, which is why these important remains were not swept away in the course of the eighteenth century to make way for something more fashionable.

A number of other Renaissance gardens, similarly grand, were created in Tudor and Stuart Norfolk. The Pastons began rebuilding their mansion at Oxnead in the reign of Henry VIII: it was a massive brick structure, arranged around three sides of a courtyard, which was further altered and added to in the next century. It had magnificent gardens, highly Italianate in flavour and carefully laid out (as at Stiffkey) in a symmetrical pattern around the hall, with terraces stretching down to the River Bure. They survive as a fine series of earthworks: so too does an impressive brick gateway, originally faced with stucco or plaster to resemble stone. A large number of classical sculptures were made for the house and grounds in the 1630s and '40s by the famous sculptor Nicholas Stone. They included statues of Venus and Cupid, Hercules, Apollo, Juno and Jupiter, and of 'the 3 headed dogd Serbros with a petestall'. There was also an elaborate stone fountain, which probably stood in the centre of the main parterre below the house. This, together with the statue of Hercules, was removed to Blickling when Oxnead was demolished in the 1730s, and can still be seen there today.

We know rather more about the gardens laid out around Raynham Hall, due to the large amount of documentary material surviving from the early seventeenth century. These are shown on a map of 1621, although they must have been only partially completed at the time and this may explain why the layout of the principal courts does not quite correspond with that of low earthworks and parchmarks revealed to the north-east of the house by aerial photographs (picture 20: although as we shall see, the gardens went on developing and the archaeological remains may, perhaps, relate to later phases of activity on the site) (28). The house stood in the centre of a geometric arrangement of courts. The one to the south-east was

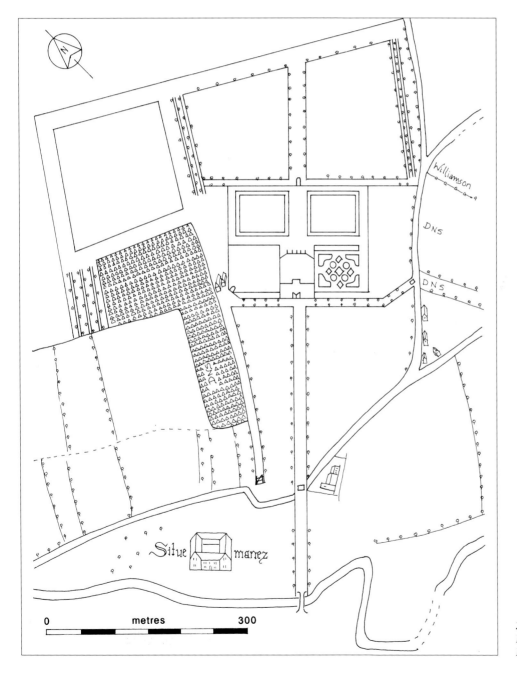

28. Detail from a map of East Raynham, 1621, showing Raynham Hall and its grounds.

presumably an ornamental garden of some kind – the map shows a parterre or knot. The enclosure that lay immediately to the north-west was probably occupied by the 'bowlinge allye' which Townshend laid out in the spring of 1621. Beyond this four-square arrangement, which covered around four hectares, there were other walks and enclosures laid out less conformably. These included a kitchen garden and an orchard. The latter was established by 1621, and contained a wide range of vegetables and soft fruit including asparagus and vines. The orchard was created slightly later: the ground was prepared in April 1621 and fruit trees – including 1,200 plums and 600 crab apples and cherries – were purchased the following year. Around the perimeter of these areas ran wide, tree-lined walks, some of which may also have been bounded by hedges of hawthorn, privet and service trees. These seem to have been high, framed features, to judge from the payments recorded in the accounts for 'tyenge the checker hedges at the upper pooles'. The entire complex covered a vast area – more than 18 hectares.

The most important symbol of status in the landscape of Tudor and Stuart Norfolk, however, was not the garden but the deer park. In medieval times parks had served primarily as venison farms or hunting grounds, although they also provided their owner with a range of other resources such as wood and timber. Enclosed from

29. The outline of the long-vanished medieval deer park at Silfield in Wymondham is still preserved in the pattern of field boundaries. Most medieval parks had this characteristic, ovoid outline.

the dwindling remnants of the once-extensive wastes, parks were usually located some way from the owner's residence, and the largest were sometimes provided with a lodge to supply accommodation during hunting trips and to provide a base for the keeper, who was responsible for the maintenance of the park and its herds. Most comprised a mixture of open grass 'launds' interspersed with more densely wooded areas, the whole surrounded by a stout deer-proof fence or 'pale'. Parks were usually roughly ovoid in form to economise on the costs of fencing (29).

The number of parks in Norfolk declined in the late Middle Ages, due to a variety of economic and environmental factors. But as they did so their location and function gradually changed. By the beginning of the seventeenth century few parks lay in isolated, remote locations. Almost all were now positioned beside great residences, proudly displayed, a fine adjunct to a mansion. Deer and the parks to contain them were an expensive luxury, and were now largely the preserve of the county elite. They were indispensable symbols of status and lordship and were increasingly treated as aesthetic rather than mainly functional landscapes. The density of trees within them was reduced, internal subdivisions removed, and more care taken of the views and prospects across them. Since medieval times many parks had contained 'standings' – towers for observing the movement of the herds before hunting – but in the course of the sixteenth and seventeenth centuries new forms of building proliferated, like the octagonal moated banqueting house (now known as the Music House) of carrstone and brick erected within Hunstanton park around 1650. At a number of sites we can see an increasing interest in the aesthetic possibilities of the park. At Hedenham, for example, an undated late seventeenth-century map shows that the park was fairly densely timbered except in the area to the east of the hall, where the trees were more thinly scattered to provide a prospect across the landscape (30).

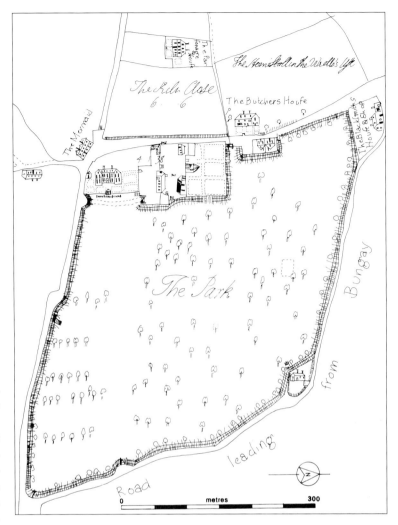

30. Hedenham Hall and park, from an undated late seventeenth-century map.

2

THE LATE SEVENTEENTH AND EARLY EIGHTEENTH CENTURIES

There was a lull in the construction of new country houses in Norfolk during the upheavals of the Civil War and Interregnum, and the exciting experiment of Raynham Hall was not immediately followed up. But the war marked a watershed in the design of large houses. After 1660 no more were built on the old pattern, ranged around three or four sides of a courtyard, entered through an imposing gatehouse. Instead, this period saw the proliferation of compact mansions that were, like Raynham, not one but two or even three rooms deep: that is, in the contemporary jargon, they were 'double-pile' or 'triple-pile' buildings. Such houses were symmetrical in external elevation and increasingly, as time wore on, in their internal layout. Moreover, the lead set by Raynham was now followed everywhere. Renaissance forms, more accurate than those of Elizabethan and Jacobean mansions, were adopted for window openings and doorways. Complex chimneys, pinnacles and pilasters, and other elaborate uses of brick now declined in favour. Houses with restrained classical details, simple outlines, regularly spaced upright windows and hipped roofs were the order of the day. These new buildings took their inspiration not only from the books produced by Italian architectural writers like Serlio and Palladio, and the innovative buildings designed before the Civil War by the great architect Inigo Jones, but also from houses on the Continent that had been seen and admired by English gentlemen seeking refuge during the difficult days of the Civil War.

'GENTLEMEN ARCHITECTS'

Indeed, this was a period particularly characterised by gifted gentlemen architects and Norfolk had more than its fair share. One was Roger North, who acquired the Rougham estate in 1693 and proceeded to modernise the existing hall there, describing his experiences in his unpublished 'Cursory Notes of Building'. North is a fascinating character – lawyer, historian and writer on many subjects – and his house was an innovative structure. This was in spite of the fact that North, who was not a tremendously wealthy man, simply adapted an existing mansion – itself a building that had been altered and added to on a number of occasions in the course of the previous two centuries – changing the layout of rooms, providing the building with a symmetrical elevation and adding an imposing Ionic portico to the south front, probably the first to be built in Norfolk and one of the earliest to be erected in England (31).

North's house was demolished by his descendant, Fountaine North, in the following century (family tradition has it that it was blown up with gunpowder). The family moved to Sussex and the estate was let. They only returned to Rougham in the

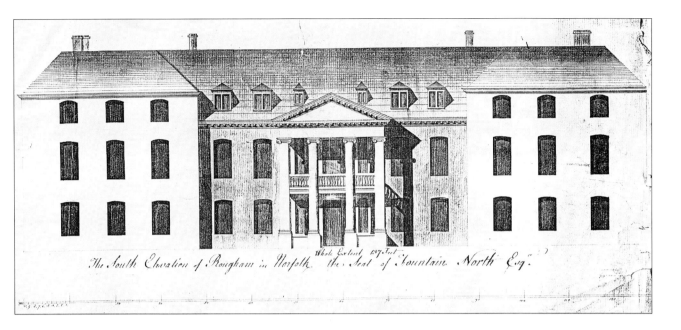

The South Elevation of Rougham in Norfolk the Seat of Fountain North Esq.

1830s, laying out a park here and living in what had been a detached service block for the hall, a building that they extended in 1878 and altered again in 1906. The basic ground plan of North's house appears in dry summers as a network of parchmarks in the turf: these can be traced on the ground but are more clearly revealed from the air (32). These traces can be compared with the plan of the hall presented in North's unpublished 'Cursory Notes' (33): and this suggests that many of the internal walls put in by North were of studwork, without foundations; and that his alterations may have involved the demolition of a line of rooms on the northern side of the old building. The somewhat chaotic arrangement of rooms revealed by both sources betrays the house's piecemeal development. Moreover, in spite of the innovative exterior, the front door opened into the lower end of the hall and although there was no screens passage, a strong memory of such a feature was preserved in the 'row of wainscote pilaster columnes screen fashion' that North placed here. Traditional ideas lingered on inside the house in spite of its innovative exterior.

Another noted gentleman architect in the county was Sir Thomas Dereham, who purchased the dissolved Premonstratensian priory of West Dereham in *c.* 1685 and, following his return from a spell as ambassador to the court of Cosimo III, Duke of Tuscany, converted the gatehouse and adjacent ranges into an imposing Italianate residence. Remains of this building still survive, although they are difficult to interpret and not easy to square with early eighteenth-century illustrations of the house (34).

The most influential of Norfolk's gentleman architects, however, was Sir Roger Pratt. Born in 1620, Pratt was educated at Oxford University and the Middle Temple and from 1643 to 1649 travelled extensively in Europe, absorbing contemporary architectural ideas. On his return to England he designed a number of houses for friends, relations and others, including Coleshill (Berkshire), Kingston Lacey (Dorset) and Horseheath (Cambridgeshire). In 1668 he retired to Ryston in Norfolk, which he had inherited the previous year. He immediately set about building a new hall, which still survives, although much altered by the architect John Soane in the 1780s. Originally – as shown in a painting of *c.* 1680 (35) – it was a nine-bay structure with a tall, three-bay block in the centre crowned by a cupola, an arrangement clearly inspired by French models. The principal floor of the house was raised above a low basement and reached by a flight of external stairs providing (in Pratt's own words)

31. Rougham Hall: the south elevation of Roger North's innovative house, designed in the late 1690s, as shown on a late eighteenth-century engraving.

27

32. Rougham Hall: the ground plan of North's house, strikingly preserved as a pattern of parchmarks in the turf of Rougham Park.

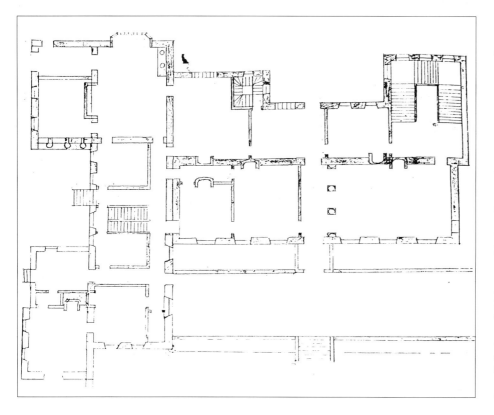

33. Roger North's plan of Rougham Hall (compare with picture 32).

Opposite, above: *34. West Dereham House, demolished in the nineteenth century: an unusual building, inspired by Italian examples, built around 1700 by Sir Thomas Dereham out of the remains of the Premonstratensian priory of West Dereham.*

Opposite: *35. Ryston Hall and gardens, as shown on an undated painting of c. 1680. The hall, designed by its owner the 'gentleman architect' Roger Pratt, still survives, although much altered by the architect John Soane in the late eighteenth century. (Courtesy Norfolk Museums Service)*

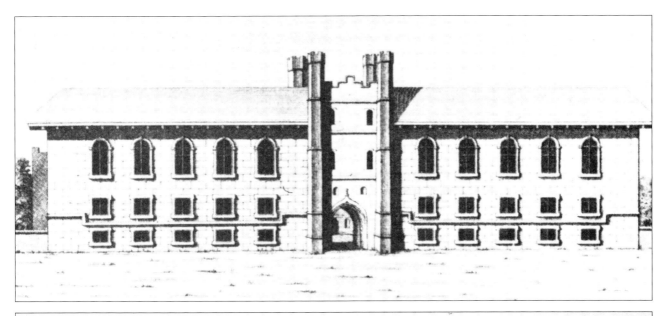

36. *Melton Constable Hall, designed by an unknown architect for Sir Jacob Astley and built in the 1670s and '80s, is the most impressive Restoration house in Norfolk. The terraced gardens are Victorian.*

'a most graceful ascent out of the court'. Pratt kept detailed accounts of the building work, which continued for several years and cost a total of £2,800.

Pratt wrote three essays on architecture, none of which was ever published. In these he discussed, among other things, the advantages and disadvantages of various kinds of house plan. Simple single-pile houses provided little privacy; courtyard plans had their advantages but were 'without all doubt, fitt only for a large family, and a great purse'. The double-pile house was the best. It provided 'much room in a little compass' and thus used up relatively little ground. In addition, it was comparatively economic in materials and – because no room had more than two outside walls – better insulated than a house of traditional, single-pile form.

RESTORATION MANSIONS

A number of houses displaying these new architectural ideas were built in Norfolk in the half-century following the Restoration: neat, symmetrical, double-pile houses with hipped roofs, and restrained classical detailing. Their internal organisation, too, differed from houses of earlier periods. Although often large they no longer included ranges of 'lodgings', for the households of great landowners were now much smaller than in the sixteenth century. The most impressive example is Melton Constable Hall, built in the 1670s and early 1680s for Sir Jacob Astley (36). It replaced an earlier manor house that stood on or near the same site. Its architect is unknown. The hall was, and is, a fairly large building of nine bays under a hipped roof: the central three bays were emphasised by a central pediment, a vaguely classical feature that was to become standard among larger Norfolk buildings in the following decades. It is built of brick but with stone dressings to doors and windows. Roger North described how Sir Jacob 'Travelled with his bricklayer, whome he used also as surveyor, to most eminent houses in England, to take patterns, and observe the mode of great houses. His caracter is avaritious, and mean spirited, and the bricklayer, for such a person, ingenious.'

As at Ryston, the main rooms were raised above a low basement and reached by an impressive external staircase. The house has been altered on a number of occasions since first built, but we can get some idea of its plan when first designed from the fine architect's model (later used as a doll's house) which is now in the Rural Life Museum at Gressenhall (37). The front door opened not into the centre of the hall, but (as at Rougham) into a residual 'cross passage', separated from the rest of the room by pillars. To the left (east) was a 'Little Parlour' with buttery behind. The principal floor also contained a Great Parlour, Withdrawing Room, and a chapel. The rooms were sumptuously decorated – the Great Chamber, now known as the Red Drawing Room, has an astonishing plaster ceiling bearing the date 1687, featuring a lavish display of flowers, fruit and game-birds. There were three staircases, a proliferation not uncommon in buildings of this status. One, with

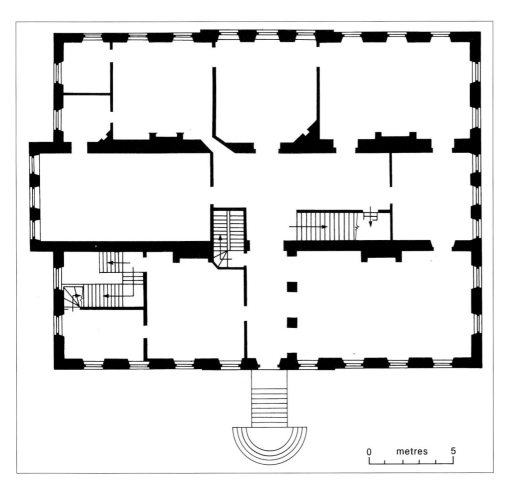

0   metres   5

37. The original plan of Melton Constable Hall, before later alterations: based on the architect's model – later used as a doll's house – in Gressenhall Museum, Norfolk. In spite of the house's up-to-date exterior, the entrance still led into a residual 'screens passage' at one end of the hall.

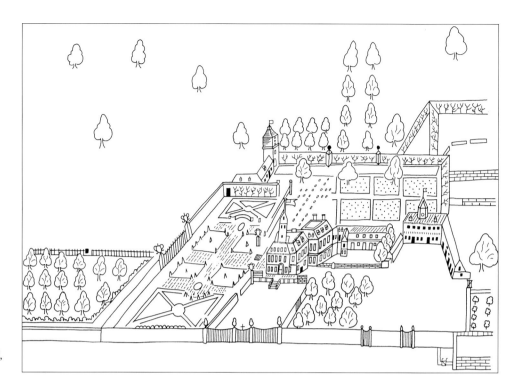

38. Buckenham Tofts Hall and its elaborate gardens in the heart of the Norfolk Breckland, as shown on a map of c. 1700.

elaborately carved balusters, was the main staircase and one was for the use of servants, who were increasingly marginalised and hidden away from the family and guests in this period: for with the disappearance of retainers and household officials only the more menial servants remained, separated by a social gulf from the polite members of the household. The third staircase provided separate access to Sir Jacob's private suite of rooms on the second floor, perhaps for when these were being used to accommodate important visitors. The building was surmounted by a tall lantern, providing views out across the gardens and estate land. This was taken down in the following century; and in the early nineteenth century the hall was considerably extended to the east.

Buckenham Tofts Hall, deep in the heart of Breckland, was a rather similar house (38). According to the historian Blomefield, during the reign of Charles II one 'Mr Vincent' built the hall and 'On the top of this house he (being a great humorist) erected a fish pond, with a bason of lead to contain the water, and had pipes of lead which brought water to an engine from a canal in the gardens, into every room (as it is said) of the house; he also built an elegant stable . . . and made a park.'

Samuel Vincent had made his fortune as an official in the government excise department. The house and its elaborate gardens are shown on a fine estate map of *c.* 1700 (38). It was a substantial structure of seven bays with a separate but connected service block. Like Melton Constable it was raised on a low terrace, and surmounted by a tall lantern, a feature that (again like Melton Constable) it was to lose later in the eighteenth century. A plan of the house, made in the early nineteenth century, suggests that its internal layout was rather more symmetrical than that of the latter house, although by this time it had been extensively remodelled – and much extended – by the Petre family, first around 1781 and again in 1803 under the direction of Samuel Wyatt. An inventory of 1809 lists no fewer than seventy rooms, including a large number of service rooms; the 1827 plan shows offices almost equalling in area the main body of the house. This feature was noted, in disparaging tone, by Roger North. Commenting on Mr Vincent's lowly origins, he observed that:

I know one bred a servant, and by accident grew rich . . . He built a house in Norfolk, and adorned it with a park, gardens and planting without, and curiosity (he thought) of finishing and furniture within. But in truth nothing was well done, but what related to servants. The capitall part of his house was paltry, but kitchen, daiery, brewhouse &c., for a duke, supposing he delighted often to visit them; but his rooms of enterteinement, as also the face and profile of the whole house abroad, such as a citizen would contrive at Hackney.

Buckenham Tofts Hall was demolished in the 1950s and its site now lies within the army's Battle Training Area.

A third large house erected in Norfolk in this period, Narford Hall, was begun in 1702 by Sir Andrew Fountaine. It was two storeys high, of seven bays, and had a three-bay, stone-faced, pedimented centre. Fountaine's son, another Andrew, was a well-known dilettante and collector who was knighted in 1699: Vice-Chamberlain to the Prince of Wales and successor to Isaac Newton at the Royal Mint, he added the stylish library to his father's house in the 1710s. Like Melton Constable and Buckenham Tofts, Narford was surmounted by a tall lantern with cupola (39). Pratt (and other contemporary writers) commended views from the roof of the house over its park and neighbouring landscape. A number of other houses from this period in the county have, or once had, balustrading around the edge of their roof, indicating a similar desire of owners and their visitors to promenade on the roof-tops, enjoying views out across the adjacent estate.

On the whole, the period following the Restoration was not a time in which many great landed families embarked on major building projects. Although renewed political stability may have encouraged building, the late seventeenth to the early eighteenth century was a time of recession in the agricultural economy. Population growth began to level off and rental incomes remained low. This situation was not helped by the institution of a new Land Tax in 1693. Those who built lavishly generally had access to some non-agricultural source of income – both Narford and Buckenham Tofts were erected by men who had made their money in government

39. Narford Hall and grounds, as drawn by Edmund Prideaux, c. 1725.

40. Ditchingham Hall, built for the Revd John James Bedingfeld in c. 1710.

service. At the other extreme, a number of leading landed families – the Pastons, Jerninghams, le Stranges and Bedingfelds – were impoverished because they had supported the Royalist cause during the Civil War, and following the Restoration had not received enough in the way of royal favours to offset the debts they had so incurred. For all these reasons, the late seventeenth and early eighteenth centuries were not, for the most part, a time in which many great building projects were initiated, although among the notable exceptions we should include the fine west range added to Felbrigg Hall, designed by William Samwell in 1675.

Nor were the smaller landowners, the local gentry, building on a very large scale, although there are many exceptions: individual family fortunes frequently buck general trends and income from the law or a judicious marriage might fund major rebuilding schemes. It is noticeable, however, that few of the families at this social level who did comprehensively rebuild their homes were still owners of the estates in question fifty years later, suggesting that grandiose ambition in this field often led in the medium or short term to family decline. Either way, the residences erected by the

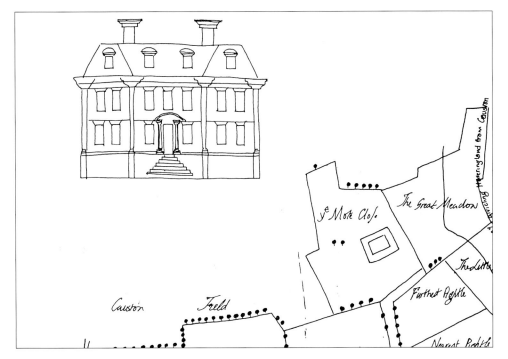

41. *Haveringland Hall, built in c. 1710 by the Herne family. The house was demolished in the nineteenth century and its appearance is only known from this marginal detail on a map of 1738.*

local gentry often betray a confident familiarity with the new principles of design. The central pediment displayed by Melton Constable and Narford became a popular feature among the local gentry in the decades after *c.* 1700. Good surviving examples include Hanworth Hall of *c.* 1700; Ditchingham Hall, built around 1710 for the Revd John James Bedingfeld (40); and Stanhoe, constructed around 1703. Some gentlemen's houses, however, had their central bays emphasised by being recessed slightly, like Aylsham Old Hall, built in the late 1680s for one of the Windhams; or Haveringland Hall, constructed around 1705 for the Herne family – the house was subsequently rebuilt on a new site and its appearance is known only from a marginal illustration on a map of 1738 (41). Some houses at this social level, however, lacked either form of emphasis, like Earsham Hall as it was originally built in *c.* 1710 (42) or Shadwell

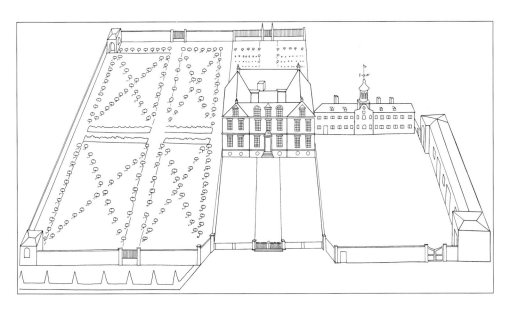

42. *Earsham Hall and gardens, as shown as a marginal illustration on an undated map of c. 1725.*

(*c.* 1727–9), both designed by yet another gifted gentleman architect of the period, John Buxton.

Moving still further down the social scale, members of the minor parish gentry were not in general building on a large scale at this time. When they did do so they tended to adopt the double-pile plan and symmetrical, classically detailed elevation of the larger houses, but the complexity of the hipped roof was often omitted in favour of the simpler arrangement of two ridged roofs in parallel. These sometimes ran parallel with the principal façade, were sometimes ranged at right angles to it. Either way, the essential element was a symmetrical elevation, usually of five or sometimes seven bays. Often such an appearance was achieved by extending an existing building. At Marlingford, for example, the Old Hall carries a datestone of 1679, but this indicates only the point at which the side wing was added to an early seventeenth-century house ranged at right angles to the road. A fine new staircase was constructed at the point where the two ranges joined. The two stepped gables facing the road obscure the true nature of the house which was not, in reality, of double-pile form, but had an L-shaped plan – although the visitor entering through the new front door, and passing through the elaborately panelled rooms, would probably have been unaware of this fact.

Many smaller gentry houses in this period were provided with shaped, curving gables on their main façades, sometimes surmounted with a pediment – so-called

43. Melton Constable Hall and its gardens, as portrayed in Johannes Kip and Leonard Knyff's Britannia Illustrata *of 1707. This is the only Norfolk mansion included in this famous collection of illustrations of country houses. Note the impossible aerial perspective: only from the air could the full magnificence of such geometric landscapes be depicted.*

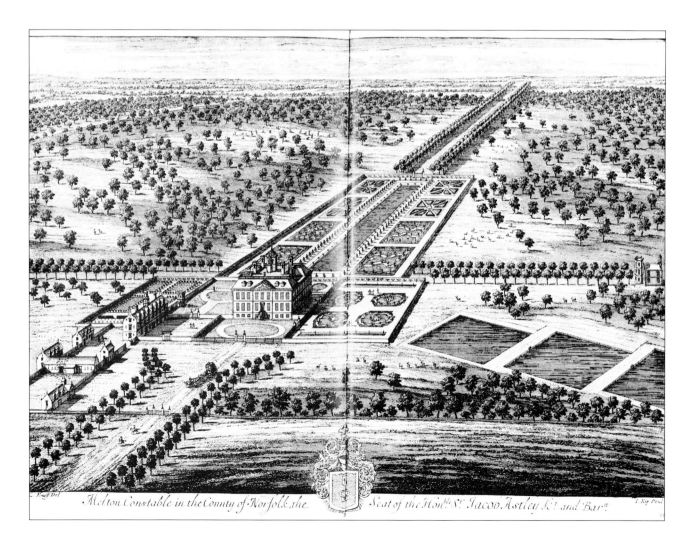

Melton Constable in the County of Norfolk, the   Seat of the Hon.ble S.r Jacob Astley K.t and Bar.t

'Dutch gables'. These forms of embellishment had appeared in the late sixteenth century. (Those ornamenting the manor house at Bracondale in Norwich, for example, were built in 1578.) They now became particularly popular and continued to be so well into the eighteenth century: Gateley Hall, built in 1726, is one notable late example. The term 'Dutch gable', which suggests that the idea was copied from the Low Countries, is not entirely satisfactory: both in Holland and in England, such forms were probably derived from published designs, like those by the Renaissance architect Vredeman de Vries, and their easterly distribution in England may owe more to the prevalence here of brick houses, to which the shaped gable was especially suited, than to the particular strengths of contacts with Europe or the immigration of Dutch refugees.

FORMAL GARDENS

The greater attention to symmetry evident in the elevations, and increasingly the plans, of country houses in this period was also apparent in their grounds. So too was the influence of France and the Low Countries. At the most fashionable residences the main axis of symmetry of the house was shared by the principal garden areas and was usually continued for some distance beyond them as an avenue. The popularity of avenues in this period reflected, in part, French influence,

44. Melton Constable today: the house and park survive but all traces of the elaborate gardens shown by Kip and Knyff have vanished. They were removed in the middle decades of the eighteenth century. The terraced gardens in the area round the hall are Victorian.

45. Aylsham Old Hall, as depicted on a painting of c. 1690.

just as the profusion of topiary and the fashion for ornamental basins or canals was to some extent inspired by Dutch designs. But we must be careful in ascribing particular features to particular foreign traditions. In practice, these various influences had become hopelessly mixed in the grounds of Europe's elites: and the same was true at a local level, as in the fine gardens created around Melton Constable Hall in the 1670s, illustrated by Johannes Kip and Leonard Knyff in their volume *Britannia Illustrata* of 1707 (43). The house stood on a raised platform, commanding a view over a large walled enclosure with a long canal running through its centre. Elaborate parterres were arranged, more or less symmetrically, down each side. These were flanked by topiaried bushes planted at regular intervals. House and gardens shared the same axis of symmetry, and the whole ensemble exuded a degree of regularity and control that was, moreover, extended out into the park and wider estate in the form of a long avenue. A weaker axis, formed by a single-planted avenue, crossed the main avenue at right angles. It led to a building called the 'Bath House', which still survives (although much altered in the 1760s) and which probably originated in the early seventeenth century as a 'standing' or hunting tower. The park itself had medieval origins. Few traces of this magnificent layout survive in the modern landscape. The formal gardens were swept away in the 1740s and the park was modified and considerably extended in the 1760s by the famous landscape designer Lancelot 'Capability' Brown, who removed the two fish-ponds to the west of the hall and created a large lake in the south of the park (44).

The gardens that complemented the hall at Buckenham Tofts were slightly less magnificent, to judge from the estate map of 1700, but impressive nevertheless,

especially for their waterworks, described by one observer as 'beautyful and delicious'. They were walled on all sides and included lawns, gravel paths and topiary, as well as a formal canal and a substantial garden building, probably created out of the remains of the redundant parish church (Buckenham Tofts, like many settlements in the arid East Anglian Breckland, had gradually dwindled in size from late medieval times). Beyond the gardens lay a walnut ground, fish-ponds and a small deer park.

Rougham, too, had an elaborate landscape. To the south of the hall an impressive avenue of lime trees aligned on the main façade of the hall still survives, although many of the trees are later replacements. Today it runs for some 600 metres but originally, to judge from an estate map surveyed in 1734 (the year of North's death), it extended outwards through the neighbouring fields for more than twice this distance: the lost southern section was planted not with lime, but with ash. Ranged either side of the avenue, immediately to the south of the site of the house, are lines of magnificent, ancient sweet chestnuts planted in a fan-like pattern. These are the remains of a formal 'wilderness', or ornamental wood. To the west of the site of the hall low earthworks and parchmarks define a large (0.8 hectare) enclosed garden of unusual trapezoidal shape, with a central pond (now a deep dry pit): this, according to one eighteenth-century visitor, contained 'every kind of fruit tree then known'. Numerous other features of interest survive in and around the park at Rougham. To the south-east of the site of the hall stands the hexagonal brick and flint dovecote designed by North, containing 999 nesting holes. It would have been visible from the main garden areas and was clearly valued as a symbol of North's status. Some

46. Aylsham Old Hall today: the elaborate barn, walled gardens and garden canal still survive in fine condition.

240 metres to the north-west of the hall – so located because of a small deposit here of impervious boulder clay – are the remains of a complex series of fish-ponds, now largely obliterated by nineteenth-century brick pits. North, among his other accomplishments, was an authority on fish and published his *Discourse of Fish and Fish Ponds* in 1713.

The great avenue at Rougham was one of many planted in the county in this period. Even quite small residences, like Aylsham Old Hall, were generally provided with one (45 and 46). Often the garden walls were punctuated with grills or 'transparent gates', so that extended prospects down the avenue were opened up. At Ryston, Sir Roger Pratt removed hedges where they obscured 'ye prospect' or, in one case, 'ye prospect of ye house towards Snow Hill and ye most graceful wood upon it'. Avenues served as a frame for the compact symmetry of the new architecture. But they were also a way of demonstrating the extent and continuity of land ownership. They were expressions of authority and control, mapping the formal geometry of the residence out across the landscape. It is noteworthy that many contemporary illustrations depict country houses from the air, in spite of the fact that no one had ever enjoyed such an aerial perspective. Only from above could the scale of a design like Melton Constable, the integration of house, garden and estate, be fully appreciated: although the tall lantern on the roof of the house would have gone some way towards providing an appropriately elevated prospect. We often forget that houses like this were originally set within very different grounds to those that surround them today: the contrast between a modern aerial view and Kip and Knyff's fanciful perspective is striking.

At the very end of the seventeenth century a new style of garden began to develop at the highest social levels, in which wide expanses of neat lawn and gravel paths were the key features, together with 'wildernesses' – ornamental shrubberies or woodland areas dissected by straight, hedged paths. The grounds of Raynham Hall were extensively remodelled in this new 'late geometric' style around 1700. A contract was drawn up for planting a new wilderness and making other changes,

47. The wilderness at Raynham Hall, as depicted by Edmund Prideaux in c. 1725. The drawing shows well the kind of simplified geometric style that became popular in the 1720s at wealthy residences.

48. *Undated earthworks, probably the remains of an early eighteenth-century garden, at Booton Hall near Cawston.*

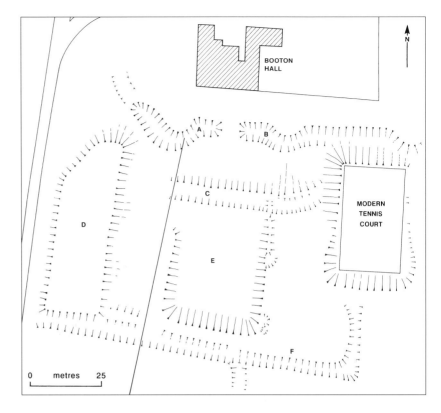

49. *The garden earthworks at Booton Hall, more clearly revealed from the air.*

works that cost the not inconsiderable sum of £460. The contract begins by describing in some detail the large amount of levelling to be undertaken to the south and west of the hall, before going on to state how the area was then to be planted as a wilderness:

> Laid into ye several works as ye Draft Prescribes, the Hedge Lines of which works to be planted with hornbeams of two sizes ye Smaller Size of about 2 foot high and Better and ye Larger Size of 4 foot high and Better: the Quarters to be planted with ye sevll. Varietys of Flowering Trees Undermentioned ye walkes to be laid all with Sand and ye Center places to be planted with Spruce and Silver Firs.

The 'Flowering Trees' to be used were lime, horse chestnut, wild service, laburnum, guelder rose, lilac, bladder senna, wild olive, 'stript' (i.e., variegated) sycamore, beech and birch. The contract also describes the changes that were to take place in the 'Parlour Garden' lying to the north-east of the hall. This was to have '4 Quarters of Grass' separated by gravel walks, and was to be surrounded by borders planted with 'A Choice Collection of ye finest sortes of Hardy Evergreens' – yews, variegated hollies, junipers, 'Cedars of Lycia', laurel and variegated box. The border next to the house, however, was to contain various kinds of flowering shrubs, including honeysuckles, syringa, citisus, hypericum, sweet briar, scorpion senna, and althea. All the borders were to be edged with '. . . some of ye Sortes of Thymes: Thrift; Pincks; or Box'. There was also to be a flower garden, enclosed from the rest of the grounds by a spruce hedge.

A quarter of a century later, in *c.* 1725, the magnificent gardens – now mature – were sketched by Edmund Prideaux (47). Prideaux's illustrations of other Norfolk seats, such as Narford, together with many contemporary maps and plans, suggest that this new, simpler form of geometric garden was widely adopted in the first decades of the eighteenth century. The plain lawns, severe clipped hedges and expanses of gravel provided a more suitable setting for the neat, symmetrical elevations of the houses they surrounded than the elaborate parterres of the kind shown by Kip and Knyff at Melton Constable. The construction of gardens in this period often, as at Raynham, involved much earth-movement, in order to create level lawns or 'plats' and terraces. The complex of earthworks to the south of Booton Hall probably represents a garden of this date (48 and 49).

In both architecture and garden design the decades either side of 1700 thus saw the growing impact of Renaissance principles of design. For the most part, however, these influences came second-hand, via France and the Low Countries. In the course of the eighteenth century, large landowners began to look more directly to Renaissance Italy for their inspiration, with momentous effects on the design of country houses and their grounds.

3
THE PALLADIAN AGE,
c. 1720–50

If the half-century following the Restoration had seen few really big houses erected in Norfolk, the next forty years were very different. In the period 1710–50 a number of stupendous residences were erected by leading county families. The first was Kimberley Hall, built by Sir John Wodehouse and designed by the prestigious architect William Talman (50). As far as the evidence goes, construction began in 1712. Kimberley was a substantial house, two and a half storeys high and with nine bays on the principal façade (five on the others). Like Melton Constable, it has a central three-bay projection surmounted by a pediment. Unlike the compact form of the former, however, Kimberley was provided with low wings flanking the central bulk of the house and connected to it by curving passages. These seem to have contained various offices and services. This was the earliest

50. Kimberley Hall was built on a virgin site by Sir John Wodehouse, to designs by William Talman. The house was begun in 1712 and comprises a central block with low, flanking wings. Its original appearance is uncertain: it was extensively remodelled in the 1750s by the architect Thomas Prowse.

example in Norfolk of such an arrangement, one that had first appeared in England some two decades earlier: it was derived from designs by the Italian Renaissance architect Palladio.

Kimberley as we see it today is rather different from the original building: indeed, its initial form is something of a mystery. Talman usually designed in more flamboyant form – he was one of England's leading Baroque architects, responsible for such imposing piles as Chatsworth in Derbyshire – and Kimberley seems surprisingly plain and austere. We know that the house was extensively rebuilt in the 1750s and it is possible that some embellishment – urns, or pilasters – were removed at this time. But the character of these changes, directed by the architect Thomas Prowse, also remains somewhat mysterious. It is clear from the surviving accounts that windows were widened and the layout of rooms altered; but these documents also suggest that the four corner turrets were added to the building at this time. These nevertheless appear, after a fashion, on Talman's original plans for the building (kept at the Royal Institute of British Architects in London) and there is scant evidence on the ground, or from the air, that they were a later addition. (Various other changes were made in the 1950s by the architect Fletcher Watson.)

PALLADIAN PILES: HOUGHTON AND HOLKHAM

The construction of Kimberley was soon followed by that of a more impressive house, Houghton Hall, built in the 1720s for Sir Robert Walpole, England's first Prime Minister. Walpole came from a family that had resided in the locality since the fourteenth century. He inherited in 1700 and was already a man of some wealth before he came to power in 1714. He used the spoils of office, however, for further aggrandisement, acquiring more land in the district, and assembling a large and compact estate. The evidence suggests that Walpole originally intended altering the existing house at Houghton before deciding, some time before 1720, to build a completely new hall on a site a few metres to the east. Work on preparing the site for this building began in 1721, the foundations were laid in May 1722 and the project had largely been completed by 1735: a fairly short time for an enterprise on this scale.

Unlike any other house in seventeenth- or eighteenth-century Norfolk Houghton was built not of brick but, in the words of one contemporary, of 'a fine white stone which is brought from Yorkshire by a sea passage of several miles and by land for 10 miles' (51). More significantly, it was the first house in the county to be built in the new 'Palladian' style, which was being patronised at the time by leading Whig politicians like Walpole. This purported to be a closer, more faithful version of classical architecture than that represented by houses like Kimberley or Melton Constable. It was also very different from the 'Baroque' of architects like Talman, a style that had been patronised by the previous political administration in England, the Tories. The Baroque was characterised by the free and flamboyant use of classical elements and ornament: it was used for rebuilding London's churches following the Great Fire of 1666 and in particular in the design of several great mansions and palaces built elsewhere in England, such as Chatsworth, Blenheim or Castle Howard. Whig theorists castigated it as symbolic of decadent, foreign absolutism. Palladianism, in contrast, involved the careful adherence to set proportions and the accurate use of classical ornament. In terms of country house architecture, the Palladians adapted the models for Italian villas developed in the previous century by the Italian architect Palladio, designs that were actually based not on the homes of the ancients, but on their temples. Houghton thus had as the central feature of its symmetrical elevation a pediment with giant, attached, Ionic columns. Moreover, following Italian practice, its principal rooms were raised up a full storey above ground level. The ground floor was called the 'rustic' by contemporaries, because –

51. *Houghton Hall was built for Sir Robert Walpole between 1721 and 1735, to designs by Colen Campbell, James Gibbs, Thomas Ripley and William Kent – as so often in this period, the precise contribution made by different architects remains unclear. Like Kimberley it comprised a central block, flanked by lower wings, connected to the main body of the house by curving colonnades: but it was built in the new Palladian style currently being patronised by the ruling Whig elite. The north wing (to the left) was designed to contain Walpole's collection of paintings. The house was built of stone, brought all the way from Ancaster in Lincolnshire. The parchmarks on the lawn in the foreground relate to a nineteenth-century garden.*

in imitation of Italian designs – it was 'rusticated', that is, its surface was made to look roughly hewn. The principal floor was known as the *piano nobile*. Like Kimberley, Houghton consisted of 'a great body and wings of vast extent' – that is, it had subsidiary pavilions, linked to the main building by curving colonnades. The view from the air brings out its formal similarities to Kimberley perhaps more clearly than that from the ground (50 and 51).

True to the ideas of Palladio, Houghton made use of a number of mathematical ratios and proportions in its plan and elevations. Thus, for example, the entrance hall is a perfect cube, 40×40×40 feet. Colen Campbell was one of the main designers of Houghton, although he may have revised earlier plans drawn up by James Gibbs. Thomas Ripley, another architect of national importance, was also involved, while the prestigious and fashionable designer William Kent was responsible for the elaborate interiors.

Visitors' reactions to Houghton varied, but few were neutral about so striking a building. Some were amazed at its grandeur; others, usually those politically hostile to Walpole, ridiculed its extravagance. To Sir John Clerk, who came here in 1733, it was a place 'full of wonders considering that it was built by a privat man'. The irascible Earl of Oxford, in contrast, was extremely negative:

> The house at Houghton has made a great deal of noise, but I think it is not deserving of it. Some admire it because it belongs to the first Minister; others envy it because it is his, and consequently rail against it. These gentlemen's praise and blame are not worth anything, because they know nothing of the art of building, or anything about it. I think it is neither magnificent nor beautiful; there is a very great expense without either judgement or taste.

The internal layout of Houghton was perhaps less novel. Like other large houses being erected at this time elsewhere in England its centre was occupied by just two large public rooms – the hall and the saloon – ranged one behind the other. These were flanked by suites of private rooms, or 'apartments', to be occupied by members of the family or visitors (52). The house was much more rigorously symmetrical in plan than Melton Constable or even Kimberley: Renaissance ideas of design had now truly triumphed.

Houghton was not occupied by Walpole on a permanent basis, for he spent most of the year in London. It was used principally for his 'Congresses', held twice a year,

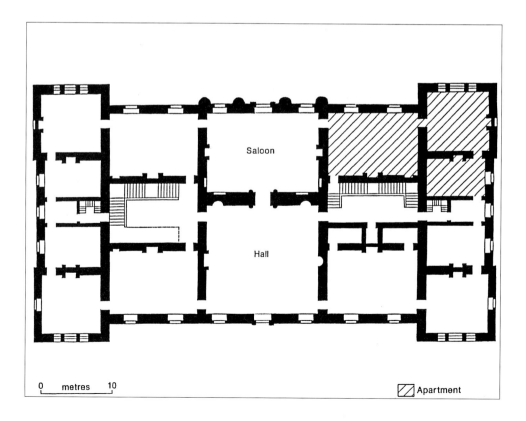

52. The internal layout of Houghton Hall as originally designed. The piano nobile comprised a number of apartments leading off from two large reception rooms, the hall and the saloon. During construction the north-eastern apartment was converted into a dining parlour and picture cabinet.

53. Houghton Hall under construction, as drawn by Edmund Prideaux in c. 1725. The low structure in front of the hall may be the cut-down remains of the original hall, used as workmen's accommodation.

to which he would invite political allies and members of the local gentry – his 'interest' – for a week of political plotting, drinking and hunting. According to Lord Hervey, the rooms in the basement or 'rustic' were the main focus of these activities: here the participants lived 'up to the chin in beef, venison, geese, turkeys etc. and generally over the chin in claret, strong beer and punch'. The *piano nobile* above, in contrast, was 'the floor of taste, expense, state and parade' – that is, where more formal receptions could take place. The rooms here were lavishly decorated.

Such rather rigid gatherings were declining in popularity at this time, however. Increasingly the fashion was for more relaxed entertaining, even at the most formal occasions, in which guests could move from room to room, dancing or conversing or playing cards, or admiring the collections of sculpture and paintings. Country house architects began to provide more rooms on the principal floor for informal entertainment and for the display of accumulated treasures. At Houghton one of the apartments was converted into a dining room while the house was being built; but it was at another new house of the period, Holkham, that the layout of rooms was most radically adapted to take account of the new social practices.

Holkham is a vast structure and took an incredibly long to time to build. It was begun in 1734, but the final touches were only being made in 1761, two years after the death of its owner and creator, Thomas Coke. He inherited the estate in 1707 at the age of ten and Holkham was administered by guardians while he went on the Grand Tour through Europe. In Italy he met William Kent and began a serious infatuation with classical antiquity and Renaissance Italy. He returned to England in

1718 and seems almost immediately to have set about planning his new house. The earliest extant design, drawn by the Norwich architect Matthew Brettingham, dates from 1726. This shows a compact building similar to, although smaller than, that which was eventually constructed, with a rustic, *piano nobile* and upper floor, and corner towers: a building, in fact, very reminiscent of Houghton. When construction finally began in 1734, however, ideas had changed. The upper storey was abandoned, so that the house had only a single floor above the rustic, and four low wings or pavilions were added. The immense edifice was built of dull yellowish-white brick, perhaps in imitation of stone, perhaps to enhance its resemblance to the villas of Italy, with their colour-washed exteriors. This final design was the work, as so often in this period, of a number of men: Coke himself, the famous Palladian architect Lord Burlington, and William Kent – different authorities disagree about their relative contributions. The actual details of construction were worked out by

54. *Holkham Hall, the largest eighteenth-century house in Norfolk, was built by Thomas Coke between 1734 and 1759. Built of dull yellow brick, perhaps in imitation of the colour-washed exteriors of Italian villas, its vast size is most clearly appreciated from the air.*

Matthew Brettingham. The immensity of the building, clear enough at ground level, is perhaps more striking from above (54).

The exterior of Holkham looks plain, even austere, although its rigid Palladian correctness appealed to contemporary architectural cognoscenti. Its interior, however, was lavish. Marble and mahogany were extensively used throughout, and the ceilings were richly gilded and carved. A particular novelty, though, was the plan of the building. Unlike other contemporary houses, it was not organised around sets of apartments leading off from hall and saloon. Instead, most of the accommodation was hived off into the peripheral pavilions and the principal floor of the main block was mainly occupied by public rooms – including a gallery for Coke's collection of classical sculpture – arranged as a circuit for public entertaining, one room opening directly onto the next (55). Such an informal plan was, in subsequent decades, to become a model for many lesser residences.

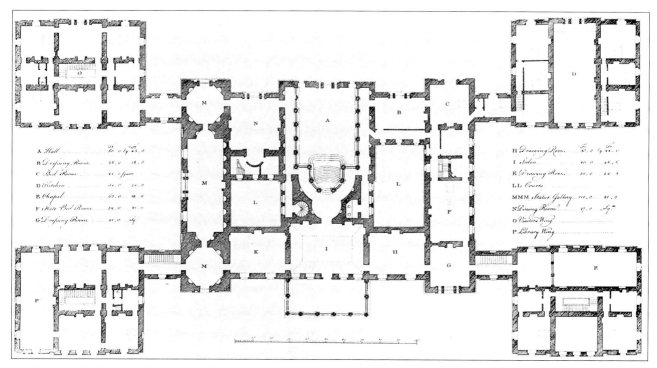

55. The plan of Holkham Hall published in Woolfe and Gandon's 1771 volume of Vitruvius Britannicus. *Most of the family accommodation was placed in the four pavilions, and the central bulk was occupied by a range of rooms for entertaining and for the display of Coke's collection of works of art. These included (to the left) a gallery for Coke's collection of classical sculpture.*

GUNTON, LANGLEY AND WOLTERTON

Most visitors were impressed by Houghton and Holkham. They were meant to be. These houses were built by two of the wealthiest and most powerful men in England. No other large properties being erected in Norfolk could match these in scale or magnificence, although several substantial houses were erected by rather less exalted individuals in this period and to varying degrees these also adopted elements of Palladio's style. Elmham Hall, North Elmham, now demolished, was built for Richard Warner in the 1720s and, like Kimberley but on a much smaller scale, had a central pediment and flanking pavilions. Gunton Hall was erected around 1742 for Sir William Harbord, and designed by Matthew Brettingham (56) the hall was considerably extended later in the century. More striking is Langley Hall, which looks like a diminutive Holkham with its prominent corner turrets, although it has two rather than four flanking pavilions (57). In fact, it achieved its present appearance over a period of time and, like Kimberley, its building history remains problematic. The corner towers were certainly a later addition, as was the central pediment, for a painting made *c.* 1745 by Francis Wooton, showing the owner, George Proctor, and a group of friends, portrays a much plainer and simpler building (58). This was presumably the 'new built mansion house and gardens which cost at least £5,000 or £6,000' referred to in the particulars drawn up in 1737 when the estate was sold by its previous owner, Richard Berney. The alterations were apparently made – probably in several stages – in the 1740s, again by Matthew Brettingham, and included many changes to the interior. As at Kimberley, what we see today is a composite structure, in spite of appearances.

Perhaps the most important house built in Norfolk in this period – after Holkham and Houghton – was Wolterton Hall, constructed between 1728 and 1741 for

56. Gunton Hall. In the foreground the original building of c. 1740, designed by the Norwich architect Matthew Brettingham. The long north range behind is a later addition of the 1780s, designed by James Wyatt, who also altered the main façade.

57. Langley Hall, like Kimberley, has a complex history. The house in its present form was designed in the 1740s for George Proctor by Matthew Brettingham, but he appears to have altered and added to an existing house, built in the previous decade for Richard Berney.

58. Painting of 'George Proctor and friends' with Langley Hall in the background. Undated, but probably c. 1745, before Brettingham's alterations to the house. (The corner turrets are not shown: compare with picture 57.) (Courtesy Norfolk Museums Service)

Horatio, 1st Lord Walpole, Robert Walpole's brother and a leading diplomat and politician. Walpole purchased the Wolterton estate in 1721. Almost immediately he began to modernise the hall and its grounds. In November 1724, however, the building was destroyed by fire (the housekeeper fleeing half-clothed from the garrets). The following month the architect Thomas Ripley – busy working at Houghton – wrote to Horatio: 'I am very sorry for your loss; but since this has Hapen'd, I think you should put an Entire stop to all your works at Woolterton; Because I believe you will a More Convenient Place to set your House in then were it now is, and to Answer your present Gardens.' The next year Ripley was commissioned to design the new hall, a building in many ways reminiscent of Houghton although without the flanking pavilions (59). Detached blocks may have been planned, and only one (the stable) actually erected, for these are shown on a fanciful elevation on a map of 1732 (60). In 1726 the remnants of the old house were cleared away and construction of the new commenced on a new site a little to the north-west of the old. The new hall was practically completed by the mid-1730s, although only finally finished in 1741.

As at Houghton or Holkham, the principal rooms were raised on a *piano nobile* above a full height rustic. The latter contained a steward's parlour, a 'common eating

59. *Wolterton Hall, designed by Thomas Ripley for Horatio Walpole (Sir Robert's brother) and built between 1726 and 1741. The balustrade and flights of stairs leading up to it, and the range to the east (right), are additions of the nineteenth century. The terrace in the foreground was designed by William Sawrey Gilpin and erected in c. 1835.*

60. *Wolterton Hall, as depicted in a marginal illustration on a map of 1732.*

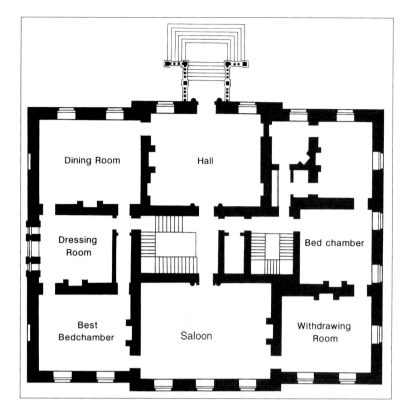

61. Wolterton Hall: internal layout of the piano nobile *as first built. (From plans in the Wolterton Hall archives).*

parlour', a library, a withdrawing room and a breakfast room. In essence, it was on this floor that Horatio and his family commonly spent their time. The first floor, in contrast, was (as at Houghton or Holkham) an area for public entertaining (61). There was a hall, with marbled floor, at the front, reached by an external flight of stairs: visitors would have entered the building at first-floor level. To the south was a saloon, on the north-west side a dining room, and on the south-east a withdrawing room. There were also two principal bedrooms, complete with dressing rooms. (There were further bedrooms on the floor above.) As at Holkham, these reception rooms were arranged in such a way that they could be used for fairly informal entertaining, opened as a circuit around a top-lit staircase.

Wolterton is a much smaller building than Houghton: Horatio himself described it as neither 'extremely large, nor little; it is neither to be envied, nor despised. The disposition of the rooms is neither magnificent nor contemptible, but convenient.' It was built to be pleasant to live in, rather than to serve as a stage for formal display, for 'parade'. This is what made it a particularly important house, for it was widely visited and members of the gentry could here see something that – unlike Houghton or Holkham – was within their means to emulate. It thus acted as a channel of ideas, through which Palladian concepts of architecture and new notions of house planning were communicated to a wide audience.

CHARLES BRIDGEMAN AND WILLIAM KENT

These striking Palladian houses were set in new kinds of landscapes. At Houghton, changes were under way even before the new hall was constructed. Maps and plans show that by the early 1720s the geometric gardens were enclosed not by a wall but by a sunken fence, or ha-ha, which allowed unrestricted views out into the surrounding parkland. The principal walks within the gardens were extended out into the park as a complex mesh of avenues (62). More dramatic changes occurred after the new house had been built. Charles Bridgeman, the leading garden designer of the day, laid out a vast and simple yet still geometric landscape, which is shown on the plan published by Isaac Ware in 1735 (63). In fact, not all the features depicted were ever created, but the essentials of the design – four great monumental vistas focused on the house – still survive today. Bridgeman extended the park, from *c.* 200 hectares to more than 300, something which involved the demolition of stables that had only recently been completed and the removal of Houghton village. This was replaced with a neat 'model' settlement: the foundations for the first of the new houses were dug in July 1729 and by 1731 it was reported that 'Sir Robert has removed about 20 houses of the Village to a considerable distance and he proposes to remove the rest. The new Building they call Newtown . . .'.

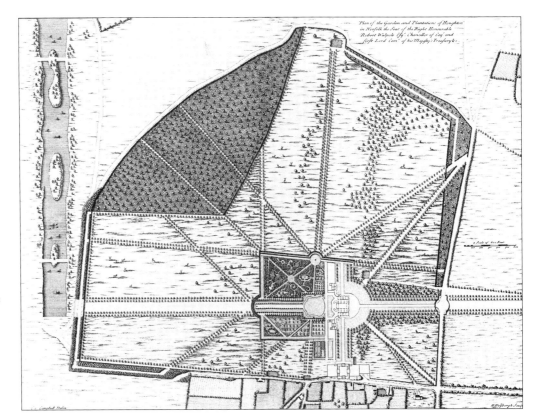

62. The grounds of Houghton Hall, as shown in Colen Campbell's Vitruvius Britannicus of 1722. The park is filled with a complex mesh of avenues, continuing the main walks and allées in the gardens and wilderness.

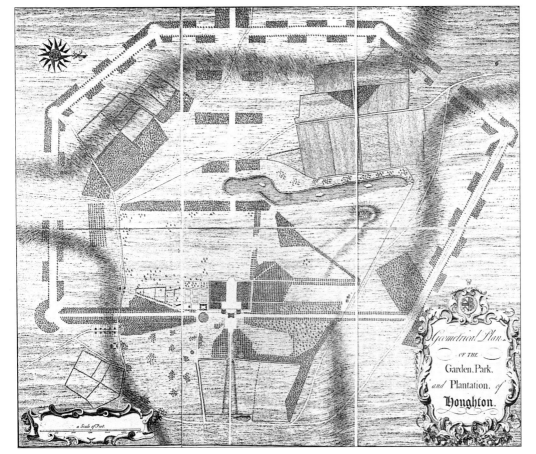

63. The grounds of Houghton Hall, as redesigned by Charles Bridgeman in c. 1728. This illustration, from Isaac Ware's The Plans, Elevations, and Sections of Houghton in Norfolk of 1735, shows a number of features that were never created – most notably, the great outer ride, reminiscent of a contemporary military fortification.

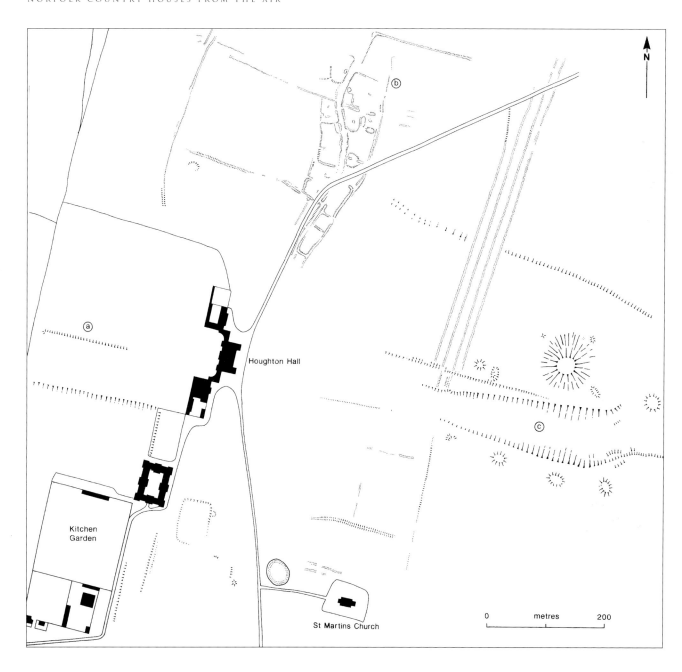

64. Earthworks in the park at Houghton: 'a', remains of the eighteenth-century garden terraces, altered in the nineteenth century; 'b', settlement remains, probably an area of Houghton village that was abandoned before the park's creation; 'c', the great cutting and associated mounds created in the 1740s.

The new village is composed of two rows of near-identical houses, with symmetrical façades, arranged on either side of a street. The remains of the old village were systematically obliterated: its archaeological traces are limited to a few low banks that mark the line of the old main street. Such meagre earthworks are in marked contrast to the settlement remains to the north of the hall, which indicate that Houghton was once – in the Middle Ages – a very large village. This is typical: villages removed in the eighteenth century to make way for spacious parks and gardens had usually already experienced much contraction (64).

Although the village was cleared away, the parish church remained. It did not survive unaltered. A visitor in 1732 commented that the 'steple' was down and soon afterwards a new tower was erected, the building extensive altered and cased in flint so as to give it a more whimsical 'gothick' appearance. It became, in effect, an ornamental building within the newly expanded park. It was not the only one. The Water House, a substantial classical structure designed by Lord Pembroke, was built around 1730 to the north-west of the hall (65 and 66). As well as forming a striking focus for the view down an avenue leading northwards from the gardens, the building also served the mundane purpose of housing the winding gear and tank that supplied the hall with water. Like the hall, it was an accurate Palladian building, with a three-bay façade of slender Tuscan pillars, rusticated ground floor and blank arches.

The landscape continued to develop into the 1740s. In particular, attention turned to the somewhat foreshortened vista to the east of the house, which was caused by a gentle rise in the level of the ground here. An undated memorandum in the estate

archives noted: 'Item: the matter of removing the hill to be decided'. A cutting was opened up, probably in 1742, nearly 100 metres wide and some 15 metres deep, but its untidy appearance suggests that it was unfinished at the time of Walpole's death in 1745. The earth taken from it was used to form a number of low mounds, which served as the base for tree clumps, and one huge mound, covering an ice house. Although there have been a number of later alterations in the landscape of Houghton, the main features of Bridgeman's design still survive. Its vast scale can, perhaps, best be appreciated from the air (67).

The grounds of Wolterton were less grandiose but developed in similar ways. The original gardens, designed in the late 1720s by the architect Thomas Ripley and the London nurseryman Joseph Carpenter, were altered and simplified from 1735, partly at least under Bridgeman's direction: a map of 1742 shows the results. A fashionable temple was erected to the east of the lake, positioned 'to take the prospect on all sides'. As at Houghton, the park was greatly expanded and the principal settlement in the parish – Wolterton Green, which lay some 700 metres to the north of the hall – removed.

There seems little doubt that the new Palladian architecture of Houghton and Wolterton, and the simple, monumental geometry of their grounds, were linked. The development of symmetrical, double- and triple-pile houses in the late seventeenth century had (as we have seen) encouraged the adoption of simpler styles of garden design, without elaborate

65. and 66. The Water House in Houghton park, designed by Lord Pembroke and erected c. 1730: view from the south (above), south elevation (below).

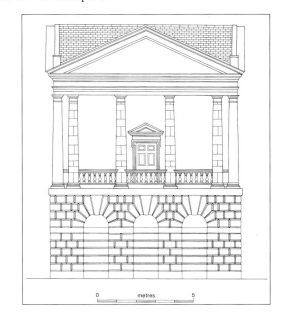

0   metres   5

67. *Houghton Park, viewed from the south. From the air the scale of Bridgeman's grand design becomes apparent. In the bottom right corner can be seen the 'model' settlement of New Houghton, built when the village was moved and the park expanded in the late 1720s. St Martin's church was left isolated within the park, and can be seen near the centre of the picture.*

parterres and numerous walled enclosures. With the arrival of Palladian houses, this development was taken further. The elegant, careful and correct elevations of such buildings invited even simpler settings of avenues and vistas which provided a frame for their elegant yet austere architecture. The design of houses and grounds was linked in other ways. In particular, the classical architecture of the mansion was mirrored outside by the erection of garden buildings in the form of temples. House and grounds together proclaimed the fact that their owner was a man of wealth, taste, power and knowledge: a member of a ruling elite for whom such things were a symbol of Britain's role as the new Rome, a nation freed from monarchical tyranny and ruled by enlightened patricians.

At Holkham, Norfolk's third great Palladian pile, the development of the grounds took a slightly different course. Here the creation of the new grounds began in 1722, even before the form of the house had been finally decided. A new landscape, in the same simplified geometric mode we have already seen at Houghton and Wolterton, was laid out around a north–south axis that was extended as an avenue for nearly 4 kilometres to the south of the hall. Where this crossed rising ground, a wilderness containing a complex mesh of straight allées was planted between 1726 and 1729, and an obelisk and temple (which still survive) was erected within it (68). The area between this and the hall was extensively levelled and its edges planted with lines of trees: holes for 473 were dug in 1726 and for a further 92 in 1727. These were staked and tied to 'lines', suggesting that they were trained in some formal pattern.

Meanwhile, work was continuing elsewhere. A new kitchen garden was built some way from the hall: and in a direct parallel with both Houghton and Wolterton the village of Holkham, which lay to the north and east of the mansion, was swept away. The large fish-ponds which had formerly existed to the south of the village were also now destroyed, drowned beneath the new lake created in 1729 by damming a natural watercourse called The Clynte. This event was followed by the creation, to the south of the site of the hall, of a smaller geometric basin, flanked by two classical pavilions or 'porches', designed by William Kent.

By the late 1730s, however, with the construction of the new house scarcely begun, the design of the grounds was drastically revised. Under the direction of William Kent the area to the south of the hall was laid out in a revolutionary new style. Instead of displaying rigid symmetry and an abundance of straight lines, the gardens were irregular and serpentine in plan (70). The geometric basin was made more irregular and naturalistic, and connected to the lake by a 'serpentine river', crossed by two bridges. A mound was raised at its western end, on the summit of which was built 'the seat on the mount' – a covered bench, like a small

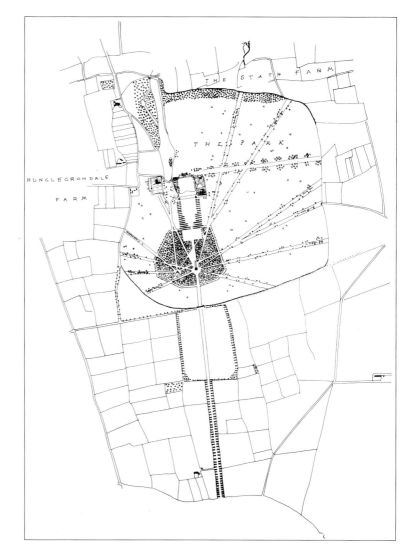

68. A map of Holkham Park, c. 1755. Although partly a proposal, this gives a good impression of the mixture of geometric and serpentine features that characterised the Holkham landscape at this time.

temple, made of Portland stone. The slopes of this artificial hillock were irregularly planted with trees and in 1742 cowslips were gathered and planted here. Outside the gardens, the lake – which had only just been completed – was given a more irregular outline and an island created within it. From 1736 onwards all the low hills and knolls within sight of the hall were embellished with plantations and clumps, and a shelter belt was established along the northern edge of the park.

Kent's drawings make it clear that what was being created in the area immediately to the south of the hall was, in essence, a three-dimensional version of the paintings by artists like Nicolas Poussin and Claude Lorraine of idealised Italian scenery. These pictures were extremely popular among landowners at the time. (A fine collection of such paintings had, indeed, been acquired by Coke himself, and were to hang in the hall on its completion.) A garden laid out as a fragment of Italian landscape represented a particularly suitable adjunct to a mansion that was itself modelled on an Italian villa. Further innovative features were added to the grounds in the 1750s, when a series of clumps was planted across the north lawn, flanking a new north lodge.

As we shall see, Kent's design only lasted for a few decades before being extensively modified, and although the basic structure of the early/mid-eighteenth-century design still dominates the landscape, much of the detail has been obscured by these and by later changes (70). Traces of the basin and serpentine river are apparent from the air in particularly dry weather, but on the ground only the slight levelled platforms where the 'porches' once stood, at either end of the basin or canal, are visible, together with the smooth contours of the 'mount' itself – so naturalistic that, if one didn't know, it could easily be mistaken for a natural landform. There are no above-ground traces of the village that once lay to the north and west of the hall. The estate accounts show that, as at Houghton, its remains were systematically levelled. Where the wealth was available, eighteenth-century landowners could

69. William Kent's design for the 'Seat on the Mount' and the South Lawn at Holkham.

obliterate a landscape as effectively as any modern town planner. The wilderness planted on the hill to the south of the house still survives, however, and within it the obelisk and temple designed by William Kent; so too does the great south avenue and the remains of Kent's clumps on the North Lawn.

The grounds around other great residences in Norfolk, such as Kimberley or Langley, seem to have developed along broadly similar lines. Parks grew in size, and garden walls were replaced by ha-has. The distinction between park and garden thus diminished; ornamental planting (especially in the form of clumps) and decorative buildings were established in the wider landscape. Avenues were reduced in number, topiary abolished, so that the mansions of the elite began to be set within landscapes of monumental simplicity, peppered with images of classical antiquity. At the same time, kitchen gardens, fish-ponds, orchards and barns were swept away from the vicinity of the house. Such landscapes expressed not only the wealth and power of their creators, and their familiarity with the culture of classical antiquity and Renaissance Italy, but also their separation from local communities and their divorce from the humdrum details of agricultural production. These developments only really occurred at the residences of the greater landowners, however. The local gentry tended to retain their walled gardens – and their farmyards, fish-ponds and barns – well into the second half of the eighteenth century. It was then that an even more radical revolution in landscape design took place.

70. Holkham Park from the south: the great south avenue leads to the obelisk, erected within Obelisk Wood in 1729–35. The photograph vividly illustrates the proximity of the park and hall to the coast. The North Sea was closer still, before the reclamation of coastal marshes here in the eighteenth century, and the lake was originally a tidal inlet.

4

AGE OF ELEGANCE: LATER GEORGIAN AND REGENCY

Few really large country houses were built in Norfolk between *c.* 1760 and 1830, although many existing ones were extended or partially rebuilt (like Blickling in the 1770s by the Ivory brothers). This was, instead, an age in which the local gentry built new homes after more than half a century of relative inactivity. For the most part, the later eighteenth century, and especially the period after *c.* 1790, saw a marked recovery in their fortunes. Agricultural prices began to rise once more as population growth resumed. This in turn led to an increase in farm rents and thus in landowners' incomes. Prices and rents soared still further in the years around 1800, because of the blockade on imported grain enforced by the French during the Napoleonic Wars. But the second half of the eighteenth century was also a period of more general economic expansion, during which England experienced a 'consumer revolution' – an enormous growth in the manufacture of fashionable mass-produced items and in the provision of services. This allowed some who had made their money in commerce and industry also to build large fashionable houses with elegant grounds, especially on the outskirts of Norwich. Yet economic and demographic growth brought problems. This was a period of increasing social tension as the rural poor got poorer, as the middling ranks of society – merchants, manufacturers, professionals – became richer and more politically assertive. All these complex and varied factors were reflected in the design of country houses and of the landscapes laid out around them.

HOMES FOR THE GENTRY

Most country houses of this period were built in a broadly 'Neoclassical' style, influenced by a growing awareness of Roman and Greek art and archaeology: architects drew on classical antiquity, rather than on the Italian Renaissance, for inspiration. The majority of houses were simple and sensible in design, and the shape and layout of rooms were determined as much by convenience as by abstract aesthetic considerations. Styles went through a number of stages but most country houses were simple and compact buildings, two or three rooms deep, usually of five or seven bays. Most were provided with a central pediment, although later this was often dispensed with, especially for smaller houses. Indeed, many of the houses built around the end of the century displayed only subdued references to classical antiquity; they were neat, rather plain structures, elegant and well proportioned. There were a few exceptions to this broad classical norm in the period before 1800, the most notable being Beeston Hall, Beeston St Lawrence, which (as we shall see) was built in a somewhat fanciful and contrived 'gothick' style.

In most of the new houses the hall was now no more than an entrance vestibule, too small to be used for entertaining. This sometimes housed a fine staircase leading to the upstairs rooms, sometimes it opened into a corridor giving access to stairs at the rear of the house. Unlike the large country houses built in the first half of the century, these more homely residences usually had their principal reception rooms on the ground floor, not raised above a basement on a *piano nobile*. There were usually several such entertaining rooms, the local gentry now emulating (in so far as they were able) the lead set earlier by mansions like Holkham or Wolterton. In this age of 'polite society', of increasing sociability among all ranks of the landed and professional classes, provision of space for informal, fashionable entertaining was essential. All houses of any importance generally had three reception rooms: a dining room, a withdrawing room, and one other – frequently a library. The dining room often led off from the left of the hall, with the drawing room on the right, which in turn gave access to the library: but there were many variations. The library increased steadily in importance in this period and as it did so its function changed from a room in which books were stored and studied to a place more generally used for quiet recreation. Other details added to the pleasure of dwelling in these houses. Full-length bow windows, providing pleasant light spaces in which to sit and read or converse, increased in popularity and there are particularly fine examples at Worstead Hall and Honing Hall.

Some of Norfolk's Georgian and Regency houses were designed by architects of national importance. John Soane, for example, undertook a number of commissions here at the start of his career in the 1780s, supplying designs for Shotesham Hall, Shadwell Hall, Letton Hall, Westgate Hall in Burnham Market and Gunthorpe Hall, as well as remodelling Pratt's house at Ryston and designing lodges for Langley Hall and an elaborate garden building, the Music House, for the grounds of Earsham. Samuel Wyatt was involved at Gunton and Buckenham Tofts. Other houses however, were designed by local architects like the Ivories (Thomas, John and William), who were responsible for the extensive alterations and additions at Blickling; William Wilkins the elder, who designed Catton Hall just to the north of Norwich; or William Wilkins the younger, who designed and later extended Keswick Hall to the south of the city. Both national and yet in a sense also local was Humphry Repton. We usually think of him as a garden designer but – with his son John Adey Repton – he was also actively involved in the design of country houses. The two worked together at Felbrigg and Barningham, while Humphry alone suggested alterations at Honing and Hoveton. One of the characteristics of this increasingly commercial age was the proliferation of professional architects and the decline in importance of the kind of gentleman dilettante – like Pratt, Buxton, Burlington, North and the rest – who had set the stylistic pace in the previous period.

Although this was not an age in which the elite of great landowners rebuilt their homes, several major residences were extended in this period and ranges extending asymmetrically to the sides or rear are a noticeable feature of many of these buildings, especially when viewed from the air – as at Melton Constable Hall, where the Astleys constructed a long service wing to the east around 1810, or Gunton Hall, where Brettingham's compact house of *c.* 1742 is dwarfed by Wyatt's rambling north range of the 1790s (56).

Fine country houses built in the later eighteenth or early nineteenth centuries can be found all over Norfolk. But they cluster around Norwich and especially in the area to the north and east of the city. In other parts of the county they are rather thinner on the ground, although the reasons for this vary from district to district. The fertile loam soils of the east of the county and the heavy clays of the south had always been characterised by relatively small properties – it was difficult to build up an extensive estate where land was relatively expensive. Moreover, many of the farmers in these areas specialised in cattle and dairying, pursuits that tended to favour the survival of the small owner-occupier to a greater extent than arable production. True, the later eighteenth century saw the steady expansion of ploughland at the expense of pasture, especially on the southern clays. But the ancient pattern of properties was only slowly changed and these remained, for the most part, areas of small or splintered freeholds, of absentee landlords and minor squires.

In the west of the county the gentry were also rather thin on the ground, but for different reasons. This area was dominated by very large landed estates like

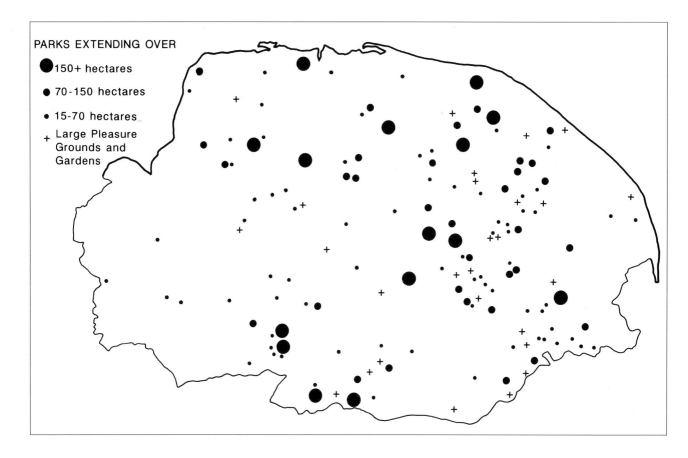

PARKS EXTENDING OVER

● 150+ hectares

● 70-150 hectares

• 15-70 hectares

+ Large Pleasure
  Grounds and
  Gardens

71. The distribution of parks in Norfolk in the late eighteenth century, from William Faden's county map, published in 1797. Parks were densely clustered in the vicinity of Norwich. In the centre-west of the county, estates were larger and the number of resident gentry therefore lower. On the fertile claylands in the south, on the fertile Flegg loams in the east, and in the Fens on the far west, there were few large landed estates.

Houghton or Holkham, properties so extensive that little room was left for smaller estates. In the area around Norwich, in contrast – and especially on the poor, light soils to the north of the city – the local gentry made money by improving their estates and increasing production to feed the buoyant urban market. It was here, too, that prosperous merchants bought properties and built fine homes within easy reach of their family businesses and other moderately wealthy people chose to reside. Here they could be within a reasonable distance of the shops, assemblies, and other attractions that the eighteenth-century city had to offer.

LANDSCAPE PARKS

This pattern is, perhaps, most clearly indicated by the distribution of landscape parks in the county, as shown on William Faden's map published in 1797 (71). By this time, all people with any serious pretensions to gentility had their homes set within a landscape of the kind made popular by Lancelot 'Capability' Brown and his numerous 'imitators'. Avenues were felled, geometric vistas softened and walled gardens removed, to be replaced by more irregular and 'naturalistic' settings. These 'landscape parks' consisted of extensive areas of turf, irregularly scattered with trees and with some small clumps or larger blocks of woodland. Classical temples or gothic ruins might be used to add interest to a view or to provide focus for a vista. Some parks contained a lake of irregular or serpentine form, and they were usually surrounded and enclosed, in whole or part, by a perimeter woodland belt. This aesthetic of sweeping irregularity required the removal of all gardens and structured detail from the principal façades of the mansion, so that the open turf of the parkland appeared to sweep uninterrupted to its walls. In reality this was an illusion:

a light iron fence, or a ha-ha (usually more discrete than those in the great gardens of the early eighteenth century), provided an unobtrusive barrier between the grazed ground of the park and the mown grass of the lawn.

Some of Norfolk's parks were created by major designers of national importance. 'Capability' Brown himself worked at Kimberley, Langley, Melton Constable and Holkham; Nathaniel Richmond, perhaps his most successful rival, designed the park at Beeston St Lawrence; Samuel Lapidge, Brown's assistant and heir to his unfinished commissions, seems to have been employed at Buckenham Tofts and perhaps at West Tofts; while William Emes, an important designer based in the West Midlands, worked at Holkham (72). Above all, the county can boast at least a dozen examples of designs by Humphry Repton, Brown's self-styled successor, who was born at Bury St Edmunds in Suffolk but who lived for a while at Sustead in Norfolk before moving to Hare Street in Essex, where he embarked on his chosen career in 1788. All these famous 'names', however, account for only a minority of Norfolk's eighteenth-century parks. Most were designed by their owners, by the estate gardener or by one of the local practitioners, usually based in Norwich, who advertised their services in the provincial press: men like William Gooch, who in 1764 informed the general public through the pages of the Norwich *Mercury* that he had:

72. Holkham: the north park, looking south. The park was greatly expanded by Thomas William Coke in the late eighteenth century, and the shape of the lake modified on two occasions: in 1782, when the north end was given a fashionable serpentine twist; and again in 1802, when the southern end was given the same treatment. The church stands alone on the edge of the park, but it was isolated long before the park was created: a map of 1596 shows that it already lay away from the village of Holkham, which once occupied the area to the west (right) of the hall.

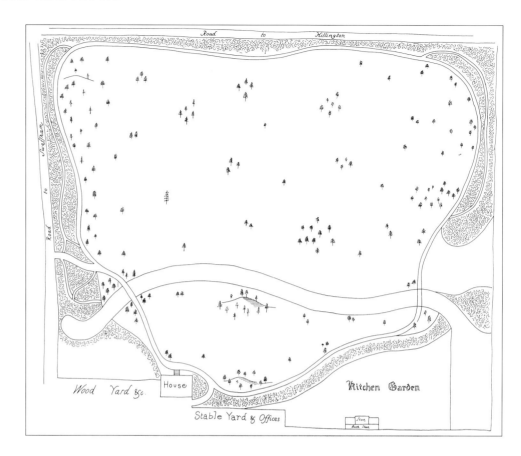

73. Hillington: unexecuted design for the park by Samuel Driver of London, c. 1773.

Now arrived from London [and] . . . settled in Norwich with an intention to undertake New Work in all its branches . . . Any Gentleman that please to make trial will find their Work faithfully executed in the neatest Manner by the above, many Years Foreman to the eminent Richard Woods, land Surveyor and Designer of New Work.

(Richard Woods was another of Brown's main rivals.) Minor designers from other parts of England also found work here, such as Samuel Driver from London, who supplied a design for Hillington park in 1773 (73).

Fashion dictated that the mansion must appear to stand solitary and isolated in extensive parkland. But in spite of what is sometimes suggested, landowners did not entirely do away with gardens and pleasure grounds in this period. At Earsham, for example, the pleasure grounds by 1770 contained an extensive shrubbery, threaded with serpentine paths, as well as a walled flower garden, separated from the shrubbery by a large greenhouse. The architect John Soane was paid for repairing the latter between 1784 and 1786 and at the same time designed an elaborate pavilion, known as the Music House, which still survives at the end of the main shrubbery walk. Gardens like this appear on a number of eighteenth-century maps. Some landowners even chose to retain parts of their old, walled gardens, as at Kirby Cane or Intwood. Such gardens were always, however, positioned to one side of the main façade, so as not to interfere with the all-important views out across open parkland.

The larger landowners, eagerly embracing the new fashion and dispensing with formal, geometric gardens, generally came to possess grounds that approximated most closely to this ideal. Their parks were normally developed by expanding earlier deer parks and generally possessed the full range of features required by the new taste, including lakes, ornamental buildings and entrance lodges. Such landscapes often had long and complex histories. At Holkham, for example, the grounds designed by Kent were drastically altered after Thomas William Coke acceded to the property in 1776. Kent's gardens to the south of the house were swept away and in the 1780s a new kitchen garden was built, some 400 metres to the west of the old, with an elaborate orangery built to a design by Samuel Wyatt at a cost of over £10,000. Through the 1780s and '90s roads were closed, the park massively extended, and around three million trees planted under the direction of the head gardener, John Sandys. The whole park was gradually surrounded by a perimeter belt and large clumps scattered across its interior. The outline of the lake was altered twice – first in 1782, by the famous designer William Emes, secondly in 1801–3, by his pupil, John Webb – in order to give it a more fashionable, serpentine shape. New lodges (many designed by Samuel Wyatt) were built, and – in the early 1790s – the Great Barn was erected in the south of the park, testifying to Coke's active involvement in agricultural improvement. While all this was going on, in 1789 Humphry Repton came to Holkham and prepared a 'Red Book' – a neat design plan with 'before' and 'after'

74. Blickling: the sombre mausoleum to the 2nd Earl of Buckinghamshire, designed by Joseph Bonomi and erected in 1794–7.

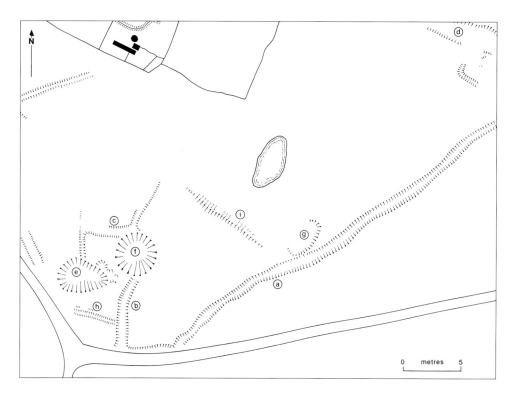

75. Great Melton Park: a typical collection of minor parkland earthworks: 'a', 'b', 'c', 'hollow ways' linear depressions marking the line of closed roads; 'e', 'f', 'g', old marl pits; 'h', 'i', former field boundaries.

watercolours of the site – outlining proposed changes to the area around the lake. These included the creation of an elaborate walk leading to a pleasure ground on the eastern shore; the construction of an elegant new boathouse on its eastern shore, to a design by Samuel Wyatt; and the establishment of a chain ferry, 'a ferry-boat of peculiar construction', leading from the new fishing pavilion to a 'snug thatched cottage . . . picturesquely embossomed in the trees', situated on the lake's western bank. Some of Repton's advice was accepted, but neither of the new buildings seems to have been erected and any activity here was dwarfed by what was happening elsewhere in the park. It is curious that Repton's rather minor contribution to the landscape is remembered by garden historians, while John Sandys is largely forgotten.

Other elite sites have similar complex history, and similar character: existing parks were expanded, lakes added or altered, and ornamental buildings scattered around the extensive grounds. Blickling, for example, by 1800 had a fine lake, a gothic 'Lady's Cottage', a 'Gothic Tower', and the sombre mausoleum to the 2nd Earl, designed by Bonomi and completed in 1797 (74). Among the local gentry, in contrast, parks usually developed from scratch: they were made by demolishing walls and yards in the vicinity of the house, by removing hedges and roads at a distance, and seeding down the area with grass. As we might expect, these landscapes generally contained fewer of the more expensive features: only a relatively small number had lakes, or ornamental buildings, for example. Indeed, the smallest examples (those in the 15–30 hectare range) were cheap and cheerful landscapes, little more than large paddocks liberally studded with trees. Often, in order to foster an illusion of size, the mansion was placed somewhat asymmetrically within the park, generally on its northern perimeter with the landscape stretching away to the south so that it could appear particularly extensive when viewed from the main, south-facing, reception rooms: this arrangement occurs, for example, at Docking, Pickenham, Colney, Booton, Kirby Cane, Catton, Intwood and Honing.

These smaller parks involved much less dramatic alterations to the landscape and were often created at no great cost. Eighteenth-century writers on garden design endlessly urged that the 'genius of the place' should be consulted when new landscapes were laid out: that the shape of natural landforms should be carefully considered, and full use made of the raw materials nature had to offer. The retention of earlier hedgerow trees was a common practice, and many parks contain ancient oak pollards that were already old when they were laid out. Such relics of the former landscape are often associated with slight earthwork banks marking the line of former hedgerows. More rarely, traces of former roads survive in the form of wide linear depressions or 'hollow ways'. Some parks, like Great Melton, contain complex collections of earthworks relating to the pre-park landscape (75).

The closure of public roads and footpaths frequently occurred when parks were created. At the start of the period this could be a complex and costly business. The landowner had to obtain a writ from the Court of Chancery or even a special parliamentary act. After 1773, however, all that was required was a Road Closure Order. This was obtained after two county magistrates had inspected the road to be closed or diverted and had declared that it was seldom used, an unnecessary charge on the parish or unsuitable for some other reason. (Any replacement, of course, was infinitely superior.) Magistrates were drawn from the same social group as the park-maker and were, as often as not, his neighbours, relatives or friends. This was a most satisfactory arrangement.

Entire villages were occasionally removed when landscape parks were laid out in the second half of the eighteenth century, but there are relatively few examples of this

76. Raynham Hall: the kitchen garden constructed in the 1780s has an unusual trapezoid shape, intended to maximise the length of warm, south-facing walls.

in Norfolk. Farms or cottages might on occasions be demolished but the most dramatic examples of village clearance – at Houghton, Holkham, and Wolterton – occurred in the period before 1750. It is true that a number of parks first created in the later eighteenth century contain earthworks of deserted settlements but in most cases these had disappeared long before the parks in question were created. At Rougham, for example, the western area of the park contains a fine collection of settlement earthworks, but these mark a lost arm of Rougham village which probably disappeared in medieval times. One or two houses were removed when Letton Park was created in the 1780s, but the earthworks that survived here until 1978 related to a settlement which had dwindled long before. At Kilverstone, too, most of the earthworks within the park are the result of medieval desertion, although a number of farms, shown near the hall on a map of 1742, were probably removed when the park was created soon after 1785. At Anmer, however, a rather larger number of cottages was apparently destroyed when the park was expanded to the north around 1803, producing a fine collection of earthworks.

The clearance of cottages and farms and, more significantly, the closure of public roads and footpaths indicate that one of the functions of landscape parks was to provide their owners with a measure of privacy and seclusion. They formed a barrier between the world of genteel leisure and that of arable production at a time when social tensions were building up in the countryside, and when landowners were beginning to have less in common with their immediate neighbours and more in common with other members of 'polite society'. The perimeter belts served to hide the views of the less attractive aspects of the surrounding countryside, especially cottages and farms. But this is not the only way in which parks demonstrated the status of established landowners. By sweeping away gardens from the main façades of the house, and emphasising the size of their parks (and thus the extent of land they could waste in non-productive uses) the local gentry and the county elite together manifested their distinctive position as landowners, very different from the middle classes who, with only a few acres of land at their disposal, continued to lay out more structured gardens, often still of a highly geometric nature.

Moreover, it was not only formal and enclosed gardens that were now removed from sight. Following the lead set earlier in the century by the greatest landowners, the local gentry now started removing dovecotes, fish-ponds, orchards, farmyards and all the other productive facilities that had formerly surrounded their homes. At all costs, the mansion should avoid looking like a farm. Kitchen gardens were tucked away behind the stables and screened by shrubberies and plantations, or more rarely, as at Beeston or Bayfield, placed in some distant recess of the park. Not that they were entirely shunned by their owners. Many contained flowers as well as vegetables, and they often formed a termination to the walks leading through the pleasure gardens: in April 1794 William Windham recorded in his diary how he had visited Holkham and 'walked before dinner into the kitchen garden'. Landowners lavished considerable amounts of money on their kitchen gardens, and experimented enthusiastically with various different shapes of walled enclosure, largely in an attempt to increase the length of the warm, south-facing walls. Some kitchen gardens, like those at Heacham, Hargham, Docking or Gillingham, adopted a trapezoid or quadrilateral form: that at Raynham, built in the 1780s, is so trapezoidal in shape that it appears in plan almost as a truncated triangle (76). Others had curved northern walls – as at Barningham, Pickenham, High House at West Acre (77) and Raveningham.

Although they purported to be landscapes of leisured inactivity, divorced from the countryside of agricultural production, parks did have some economic uses which helped offset the costs of their creation and maintenance. Sheep and cattle were grazed in them, and woods and plantations were managed with profit as well as beauty in mind. But economic functions were always carefully combined with the needs of recreation. Game-shooting increased steadily in popularity: William Marshall in 1782 noted of Norfolk that the 'Ornamental plantations, about the residences of men of

fortune, are here, as in other districts fashionable; not, however, as objects of ornament merely, but likewise as nurseries of game.' Similarly, lakes were not simply intended to improve the view from the mansion. They were used for boating and for fishing. Such pastimes were not restricted to the owner and his family, but were available to guests and visitors. Indeed, the larger landscapes were often open to all who appeared respectable – at least on specified days. Holkham park, for example, was open to the public from 1760 at least: 'every Tuesday, but no other day. No persons will be admitted that do not tell their names.' By 1788 it was open every Thursday in July and August, and Repton in his Red Book of 1789 refers to the importance of making sure that the boats on the lake were 'properly rigg'd and dress'd in their colours on public days'. At one level the park was a landscape of seclusion, deigned to exclude the poor. But at another it was a landscape for sociable entertainment, for the enjoyment of the 'polite'.

The casual elegance of the landscape park, and the refined simplicity of the eighteenth-century country house, complemented each other perfectly. Moreover, the internal organisation of the house was mirrored in the layout of the landscape. When houses had been laid out on formal axes it was natural that these should be extended out into the surrounding grounds in the form of straight gravel paths and avenues. Now that more flowing, circulatory plans had become fashionable, people came to enjoy the views out of the house and towards it from a number of slowly changing perspectives,

77. The kitchen garden High House, West Acre, shows another way of increasing the length of warm, south-facing wall: the north wall, added to the existing garden in the nineteenth century, has an elegant curve.

rather than down rigidly defined avenues and vistas. The meandering paths in the pleasure grounds, and the more extended serpentine drives running through the parks, were – like the more flowing spaces created within the house itself – well suited to the kind of informal entertaining now popular among the gentry and greater landowners in this age of elegant informality. House and grounds often developed side by side at the same time. Edmund Rolfe kept a detailed account of the 'Various Expenses in the Improvements at Heacham begun in 1768', which provides a fascinating insight into the economics of country house building. The park here cost no less than £913 5s 1d to create, a large sum but spread over a period of eight years. Its creation overlapped with that of the kitchen garden, which itself cost £898 7s 0d – much of which went on the 481,000 bricks used in its walls and greenhouses. Work on the hall began in 1774, Rolfe adding a smart new range to an existing building. The total cost was £4,128: a further £1,025 went on the fittings, which included matching wallpaper and chinz curtains, mahogany furniture and marble fireplaces.

HONING HALL

Norfolk has many fine houses and parks of this period and a few examples will serve to convey something of the flavour of the age. We may begin with Honing Hall, first built around 1748 by Andrew Chamber, a prosperous member of the local gentry (78). It replaced an earlier house, shown on a map of 1728, which stood on an immediately adjacent site. The new house was a rather plain red-brick structure of five bays and with a central pediment of three bays. It initially had a plan typical of the first half of the century, with a large entrance hall but only one other decent-sized reception room, situated on the ground floor in the north-eastern corner of the building. The estate did not remain in the hands of the family for long. Chamber's son fell into financial difficulties and was forced to sell in 1784. It was purchased by the elderly Thomas Cubitt, a member of a family which had long been prominent in the local area. His son, another Thomas, was a lawyer based in London who was engaged to the daughter of Henry Spencer, a wealthy London merchant. On their marriage in 1785 they moved into the hall and in 1788 began to make improvements, commissioning the architect John Soane to draw up plans. The entrance hall was to be reduced in size, allowing a small ante-room to be created behind it, giving access to a new flight of stairs. At the same time a larger room was to be formed in the north-west of the house by amalgamating a smaller chamber with the space occupied by the now redundant staircase. Such an arrangement would have produced a more fashionable plan, with a fine entrance hall and two large reception rooms at ground-floor level, and with a staircase rising up through the centre of the house. In fact, these precise alterations were never carried out, although the large north-western room was created, and provided with another fashionable feature of the period: a full-height bow window overlooking the garden, a very fine feature.

Further alterations were envisaged in 1792, when Humphry Repton was called in to advise on the house and its grounds. The modifications carried out to the house were relatively minor, relating only to its external appearance: Repton provided it with a parapet, and with a white string course beneath the first-floor windows. More significant were the changes he proposed for the grounds. A park had already been established here, probably in the 1780s, and Repton advised against greatly extending it because this would create a landscape out of keeping with the dimensions and status of the house – one of Repton's perennial concerns. Only to the south should expansion occur, 'if the hill field belonging to Lord Orford could be obtained': a tower might then be erected on the summit of the hill to act as an eyecatcher. He also suggested that a new entrance drive should be provided, leading into the park from the west, and that the kitchen garden should be reduced in size, and screened from the house by a plantation. Most significantly, he suggested changes to the eastern entrance. Repton, who was always concerned with the effect that first impressions would make upon the visitor, suggested that the straight road forming the eastern boundary to the park and the right-angle entrance leading off from it diminished the grandeur of the house, because the road seemed 'to lead to some other place of greater importance beyond it'. Instead, the drive should leave the road in a gentle, smooth curve in order to foster the impression that the public road was leading directly (or at least principally) to Honing Hall. The status of the entrance should also be enhanced by a lodge. Most of Repton's suggestions – with the exception of those relating to the eastern entrance – seem to have been carried out, although some (especially the expansion of the park south-westwards) took some time to achieve. There have been few subsequent alterations and the hall and its grounds, which are still owned by the Cubitt family, give a superb impression of a small eighteenth-century gentleman's residence.

78. Honing Hall was built in the 1740s and altered in the 1790s with, among other things, the addition of the full-height bow window on the garden front. The house sits on the northern edge of a particularly fine park designed by Humphry Repton.

LETTON, SHOTESHAM AND RAVENINGHAM

Letton Hall (79) is rather later in date. Designed by the architect Sir John Soane, it was built between 1785 and 1788 and replaced an earlier house that stood slightly to the north-west. The new mansion – which was built of white brick – was the earliest large house to be designed by the architect and was in a rather severe Neoclassical style. It has five bays on each side and is two and a half storeys high, with a low parapet all around and a central pediment on the east front. It has arched windows on the ground and first floors. Unfortunately there have been a number of subsequent alterations to the house. It was extended in the nineteenth century and the south entrance front rebuilt, although the classical Tuscan columns of the original porch were reused. Soane's entrance hall survives, however; rectangular with apsed ends, this – as in many houses of the period – contains a fine staircase, lit from a skylight above.

A diminutive 'park' – a small area of well-timbered pasture – had existed to the south of the previous hall but this was greatly extended following a Road Closure Order of 1791, which diverted the Cranworth road to the south. Interestingly, the map accompanying the closure document shows that the lodge, which still stands beside this new road, had already been built before the order was passed – a clear sign that no opposition to the proposed diversion was expected. The common that lay to the north and east of the hall – Letton Green – was enclosed and incorporated within the park, together with the adjacent fields. A number of farms and cottages

79. Letton Hall, designed by John Soane and built between 1785 and 1788, replaced an earlier house that stood slightly to the north-west. The new mansion is of white brick in a rather severe classical style: it has been altered on a number of subsequent occasions, and the terraced gardens are nineteenth-century additions, but Letton nevertheless gives a good impression of a medium-sized late Georgian country house.

80. *Shotesham is another Soane house, built in the in the 1780s on a virgin site, replacing an earlier hall that stood c. 1.4 kilometres to the east. It is a compact Neoclassical building of four bays on the main façade, with 'giant' pilasters (i.e., running the full height of the walls) spaced at regular intervals and windows set in recessed arches. The kitchen garden, also designed by Soane, lies to the north, surrounded by a screen of shrubbery. The stables are discreetly hidden away to the rear.*

81. Raveningham Hall was built on a virgin site in the late 1770s, close to the parish church that already lay almost entirely isolated. The park was laid out around the same time, and contains a number of magnificent ancient oaks, incorporated from earlier hedgerows.

standing beside the green were removed although, as noted above, the settlement here had already declined considerably since medieval times.

Some of the new houses erected by the gentry in the course of the eighteenth century were, unlike Honing or Letton, built on virgin sites, some distance from their predecessors. Shotesham Hall to the south of Norwich is one example (80). It was erected – again to designs by Soane – in the 1780s, some 1.4 kilometres to the west of what became the Old Hall. Soane prepared two plans for the house. The one chosen was for a compact building of only four bays on the main façade, with 'giant' pilasters (i.e., running the full height of the walls) spaced at regular intervals and windows set in recessed arches. In Soane's words, it was built in the form 'of half the letter H and is fronted with white bricks of the best quality', and had details in Portland stone and the new artificial 'Coade Stone'. Its internal plan was rather old-fashioned, with a great staircase occupying much of the centre of the building, but it had three large reception rooms, all of similar size – a library, a withdrawing room and a dining room. A new park was laid out around the time the

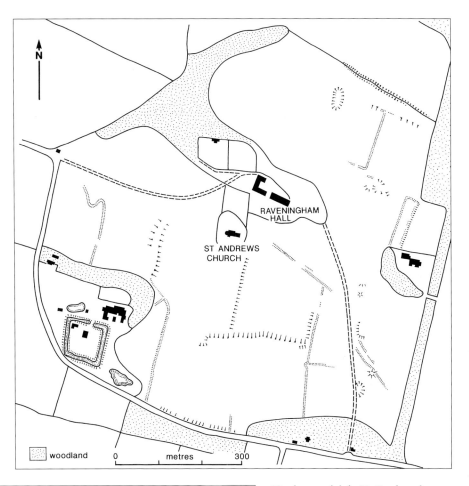

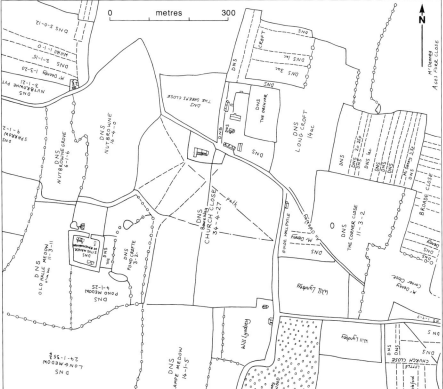

82, above and, left, 83. Earthwork features in Raveningham park – most of the lost roads and field boundaries can be correlated with features shown on a map surveyed in 1632, long before the park was created.

hall was erected. It covered an area of over 100 hectares on the sloping ground to the east of the River Tas and had woodland belts around much of its perimeter: the hall lay close to its centre. The kitchen garden was a little to the north, surrounded by pleasure ground and shrubberies. It was apparently designed by Soane himself and he prepared a planting plan showing the positions of the fruit trees – forty-nine different varieties in all.

Raveningham Hall was also built on a virgin site, probably in the late 1770s: the previous house stood on a moated site, which still survives to the south-west of the park (81). The parish church of St Andrew, with its round tower, stands 100 metres to the south-west of the hall but it does not mark the site of a village cleared away when the park was laid out: a map of 1632 shows that – like many churches in this part of Norfolk – it was already virtually isolated, settlement having drifted away from it during the early Middle Ages.

The new hall was a substantial brick structure of seven bays and two and a half storeys, and with a central pediment extending over the central three bays, projecting forwards slightly from the rest of the building. Originally it had two low wings. It was built by Edmund Bacon, who came from nearby Gillingham and acquired the Raveningham estate through his marriage to Mary Castell, whose family had lived there since medieval times. The house was extensively altered at the end of the nineteenth century by the architect Somers Clerk, who, among other changes, added a four-bay portico to the north front, together with a fine circular window and bow windows at first-floor level. The side wings were also enlarged at this time, but they were taken down in the 1940s.

The fine park was laid out in the early 1780s: a road running east–west immediately to the south of the hall was diverted by a Road Closure Order of 1783, and the accompanying map shows that at this time the surrounding land was still divided into hedged fields. The road was relaid to the south, around the boundary of the new park, and a number of new plantations were established. Like most landscape parks, however, Raveningham made extensive use of pre-existing trees, and is still dotted with a number of massive pollarded oaks, some with girths in excess of 7 metres – among the finest 'veteran trees' in Norfolk. Most had been growing within hedgerows and the park contains a number of low earthworks marking the line of former field boundaries and long-abandoned roads, most of which can be correlated with features shown on the 1632 map (82 and 83). The park is not a large one – covering c. 70 hectares, it was about average for a moderately wealthy family. Nevertheless, like most parks it provided its owners with a degree of privacy and exclusivity, an impression vividly conveyed by an aerial perspective.

GOTHIC ELEGANCE: BEESTON HALL

Almost all the new houses of the eighteenth century were built in some broadly classical style, but Beeston Hall, Beeston St Lawrence, is a notable exception. It was erected by Jacob Preston, who inherited the estate in 1769. Preston was a fairly wealthy landowner with a rental income of more than £11,000 per annum and other investment income much exceeding this. He was also a well-educated individual who completed the Grand Tour and who was elected a Fellow of the Society of Antiquaries. To begin with, Preston was content to add a new front to the existing hall at Beeston, in the new (and somewhat revolutionary) 'gothick' style. But soon afterwards he decided to rebuild the house altogether, probably because the existing hall was in a valley, 'situate rather low, with a piece of water at the bottom'. The new hall, erected slightly higher up the valley side, was and is a striking structure with pointed windows and battlements. It is, however, somewhat restrained in appearance, ornate rather than picturesque (84). This is largely due to

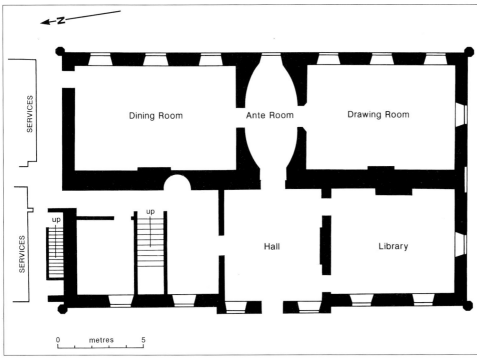

84. Most eighteenth-century Norfolk houses were built in a loosely classical style: Beeston Hall, built for Sir Jacob Preston around 1786, is an exception: a restrained, symmetrical, 'gothick' house, faced in knapped flint.

85. The internal layout of Beeston Hall (after Nigel Wright).

the fact that in spite of the pseudo-medieval details it has a precise, symmetrical elevation like contemporary houses in the more usual classical style, with seven bays and a central three-bay projection. The interior, too, is largely symmetrical (85). The house is faced with knapped flint, a choice that cost Preston a great deal of money – around three times the price of the more usual white brick. The designer is unknown, but was possibly William Wilkins the elder, a leading local architect.

The house's internal decoration was more varied than its external appearance. The library is in a gothic mode, and the hall has a vaulted and ribbed ceiling of vaguely medieval inspiration. But the rooms along the south side of the house – the drawing room, dining room and the oval ante-room linking the two – are in a chaste classical style.

Surviving bills are incomplete but they suggest that the hall cost well over £1,000 to build. Large sums were also spent on the surrounding landscape. A park of some kind already existed at Beeston but Preston commissioned one of the leading landscape gardeners of the day, Nathaniel Richmond, to prepare a design. Much new planting was undertaken, a lake created and the old walled gardens in the

86. Beeston Hall stands within the degraded remains of a fine park, designed in the 1770s by one of the country's leading landscape gardeners, Nathaniel Richmond. The lake in the foreground is by him, and it was probably his decision to rebuild the kitchen garden in an isolated position, some way to the north of the hall – one of comparatively few examples of this practice in Norfolk.

vicinity of the hall swept away. At least one visitor, however – Preston's brother-in-law, Henry Hulton – was unimpressed with this last change, writing to his sister how Preston:

> had one of the gentlemen improvers here to modernise his grounds and is busy levelling his lawns, removing gardens, walls and trees, and laying down a new kitchen garden more remote from the house. It would grieve you if you were here to have such a fine kitchen garden cut up . . . and laid to lawn, but so it must be, our ideas are more extensive than those of our ancestors. They were cribbed up in small apartments, and sat in little cane chairs admiring the pretty enclosed garden edged with box and yew trees. We now indulge in elbow chairs, in apartments 20' by 30' by 15' high, and must extend our view over improved grounds as far as the eye can see without any disagreeable object intervening.

The new kitchen garden to which Hulton refers – one of the few in Norfolk which really *is* lost in the recesses of the park – still survives some 200 metres to the north of the hall, hidden behind a screen of trees and shrubs (86).

Preston never really lived in his new mansion. He and his family stayed at their house in London for most of the time that the building work continued. He fell from his horse and was killed in 1787 while riding to inspect the progress of another great building project with which he was involved: the construction of the new workhouse at Smallburgh.

REPTON'S FIRST AND LAST COMMISSIONS: CATTON AND SHERINGHAM

All the houses so far discussed were built for members of the established landed gentry and replaced earlier manor houses. Catton, in contrast, was an entirely new creation, built with 'new' money on a virgin site in what was then a small village a little to the north of Norwich. It was begun in 1788, its owner Jeremiah Ives having purchased property here a few years earlier. Ives was a prosperous textile merchant whose father, grandfather, great-uncle and cousin all served as mayors of Norwich, and whose sisters married into the leading merchant, manufacturing and banking families of the day. Catton was already on its way to becoming a fashionable suburb, with a number of new houses set in diminutive parks. The late eighteenth-century historian Armstrong described it as a 'Very pleasant village, and the residence of many opulent manufacturers, who have retired from Norwich, and built elegant houses. The air is reckoned very healthful, and many invalids resort thither for the benefit of it.'

The house was probably designed by William Wilkins the elder, a local architect. It is a rather dull structure, typical of its period, without a central pediment but with two large bows arranged symmetrically on its southern elevation. The most interesting feature of Catton is, in fact, the park, which was designed in 1788 by Humphry Repton as his first paid commission (87). Ives did not possess a country estate in the traditional sense. He owned, in fact, no more than a few fields, and the site chosen for the house (probably by Repton) typically lay at the northern end of the property, on rising ground overlooking Norwich, with the park sloping away to the south. Repton, from the very start of his career, was an expert in visual illusion: the perimeter belts of beech, oak and sweet chestnut were carefully contrived in order to allow selected views out into the few fields actually owned by Ives, which Repton planted up in a suitably ornamental fashion, to give an impression of a large and continuous estate. The village itself, which lay immediately to the north of the house, was carefully screened by dense planting, although again there was a gap – to

87. Catton Hall was designed by William Wilkins, a local architect, and its park laid out by Humphry Repton, as his first paid commission. The park was extended to the south and west in the 1850s, and the line of the original belt can clearly be seen, marked by a line of trees. The site is now in multiple ownership, and – as this aerial view clearly indicates – engulfed in the suburbs of north Norwich.

ensure that the tower of the parish church, picturesquely covered with ivy, was in full view of the pleasure ground. In addition, a small picturesque thatched cottage was placed at the eastern end of the village, near the entrance to the park: nestling in a deferential way at the gates, it helped to give the misleading impression that the entire village was Ives's property.

Catton park as we see it today is not exactly as Repton left it. Ives's widow sold the estate in 1835 to one Captain George Morse, on whose death in 1852 it was purchased by John Henry Gurney. A few years later the house was extended, the park was expanded to the west and a new southern drive created. A new belt was established, Repton's original belt thinned and various other alterations undertaken. The line of Repton's old western belt is still apparent from the air as a line of trees running diagonally across the park's south-western corner. The estate passed to the Buxton family in 1866 and the hall was bought by Norfolk County Council in 1948 and used as a nursing home. The house is now in private hands: the park survives in divided ownership, in degraded condition, and – as picture 87 shows – is now engulfed on all sides by the suburbs of north Norwich.

The houses and parks of the period from 1750 to 1820 give a fairly clear message. They indicate the continuing wealth and importance of the greatest landowning

families, but also the rising fortunes of the gentry and the success of some manufacturers and merchants. The houses of the period were pleasant, elegant places, well suited to informal sociability, and the parks laid out around them were in a style that was shared by the landed elite, and the squirearchy. All the propertied classes were now mixing together in an affable way, and the casual elegance of houses and pleasure grounds was in a sense a mirror of this 'polite society'. Yet at the same time, by clearing away cottages, removing roads and planting perimeter belts, the rich expressed their divorce from the communities around them and created landscapes for private recreation. Only at the very end of the century did increasing unease about social tensions, heightened by the bloody events of the French Revolution, lead some writers on landscape design – most notably, Humphry Repton – to advocate the creation of less exclusive and secluded settings for the homes of the wealthy.

Sheringham was Repton's last commission. The house – a compact two-storey building with simple windows, a porch with Tuscan pillars and a veranda on the south side – was designed jointly with his son John Adey Repton and built between 1812 and 1817. It is now the property of the National Trust (88). The existing park was greatly embellished by Repton, with some input from the owner

88. Sheringham Hall was designed by Humphry Repton and his son John Adey Repton in 1816. Humphry also designed the park, his last commission and one that he was particularly pleased with, although he adapted a number of existing features in the landscape. Repton also chose the site for the house, nicely sheltered from the sea winds by the wooded rise to the north. The property is now owned by the National Trust.

Abbot Upcher, and the 'Red Book' he prepared shows clearly enough his increasing desire to create landscapes that would express the landowner's paternal concern for the local poor. The park was small but Repton advised against 'extending the verdant surfaces too far' on the grounds that he considered 'The mixture of corn-lands with woods, at a distance, more cheerful than grass, because, at certain seasons, at seed-time and at harvest, it may be enlivened by men as well as beasts.'

This was not to be a landscape hermetically sealed from the world of agricultural production. Indeed, Repton lamented the 'Modern fashion of placing the house in the middle of a park, at a distance from all mankind', contrasting this with the time when 'the country gentleman's seat' had only been 'separated from his neighbours and dependants by court-yards and garden-walls'. He suggested that the poor should be admitted, 'under the eye of the keeper', into the park woods once a month in order to gather fallen boughs. Where this practice had been adopted, he argued, 'no wood is stolen, and no trees are lopped and disfigured'. He even advocated the adoption of certain recreational activities on the estate through which social tensions might be dissolved. Thus, he suggested, coursing was preferable to shooting: 'One is a selfish, the other a social, enjoyment. The villagers will occasionally partake in the sport . . . thus promoting a mutual endearment betwixt the landlord, the tenant, and the labourer, which is kept up with little expense, securing the reciprocity of assistance of each to the other.' But to a large extent advice like this fell on deaf ears. If anything, the grounds of Norfolk landowners' houses became even more enclosed and private in the course of the nineteenth century.

5
THE NINETEENTH CENTURY

In Norfolk, as elsewhere in England, country houses continued to be erected on a large scale throughout the nineteenth century. While many of these buildings – like Stow Bardolph or Costessey – were the homes of established landed families, others were created by new recruits to the landed elite from the world of finance, trade and industry. Lynford, for example, was built for Mr Lyne Stephens, 'the richest commoner in England', and his wife, a French ballet dancer. Our understanding and appreciation of the houses of this period are somewhat distorted by the fact that several of the largest and most magnificent piles, designed by some famous architects, have been lost: houses like Haveringland, designed by Edward Blore in 1839 and demolished in 1946 (89); Bylaugh, by Charles Barry, which was largely demolished a century after its completion in 1852 (thereby, it was said, fulfilling a curse); or Costessey,

89. Haveringland Hall, the great Italianate mansion designed by the architect Edward Blore, completed in 1852 but demolished less than a century later. (Drawing by Alan Mackley)

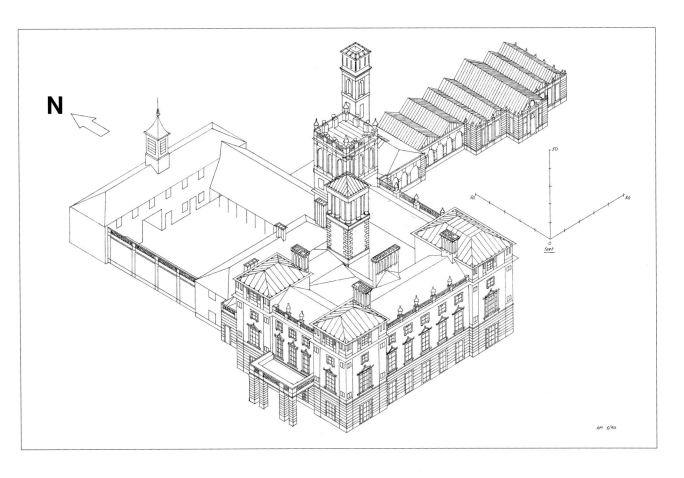

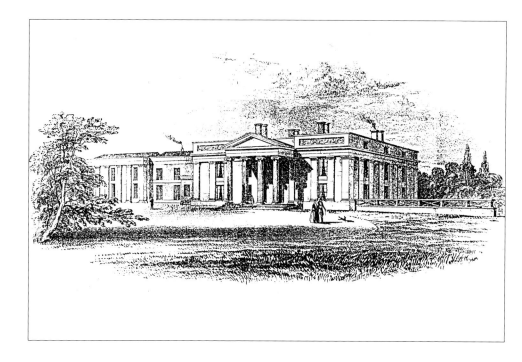

90. South Pickenham Hall: two illustrations from a sales catalogue of 1843 show Donthorne's Neoclassical house as it was before drastic remodelling at the start of the twentieth century.

designed by J.C. Buckler and built over many years between *c*. 1830 and *c*. 1860.

We perhaps pay the houses of this period less attention than we should. They are often castigated as dull and derivative, and it is true that their styles were based on the fashions of previous centuries: this was an age of diverse historical revivals. But they developed and altered these originals in new ways, and it is unlikely that we would ever mistake the nineteenth-century revival for the real thing. In contrast to the previous century, no particular style was now universally favoured. Some owners, especially in the 1820s and '30s, chose the 'Greek Revival' – a style influenced by a growing interest in Greek, as opposed to Roman (or Renaissance), art and architecture. A few built in 'Italianate' mode, that is, following the pattern of seventeenth- and eighteenth-century Italian palaces – the lost Haveringland being the most impressive example (89). In Norfolk, however, these styles were never as popular as in some other regions of England and most landowners preferred indigenous antiquarian styles: gothic, Jacobean or Elizabethan.

DONTHORNE'S HOUSES

Individual designers often worked easily in several styles. One important example was W.J. Donthorne (1799–1859), an architect of national importance who was born (the son of a hatter) at Swaffham in 1799. He initially trained in London with the prestigious architect Jeffry Wyattville, and his first buildings – like Hillington Hall or Cromer Hall – were in a gothic style. But he also built or modified houses in a Neoclassical, 'Greek Revival' mode (Wallington Hall, Elmham Hall, High House at West Acre and Pickenham Hall in South Pickenham). His unexecuted scheme for Felbrigg Hall in 1825 would have created new reception rooms decked out in a whole range of current architectural fashions: classical, gothic and Jacobean!

Few examples of Greek Revival houses survive in Norfolk from this period and Donthorne's essays in this style have fared particularly badly. His alterations to Elmham Hall disappeared with that building's demolition in 1925; while West Acre

High House (77) was remodelled in gothic style in the 1880s. Pickenham Hall, South Pickenham, was also later rebuilt (in the early twentieth century) but much is known about its earlier plan and appearance (90). Here, as at many other places, the nineteenth-century changes involved both drastic alterations to and the substantial extension of a smaller building: in this case, a small Palladian house of the 1770s. Donthorne was commissioned to update this structure by William Wigget-Chute in 1829 and the result was a building of 'chaste and classical elevation', with a substantial portico on its western side and prominent pilasters (characteristic of the style) all along its principle elevations. A new range was added to the north, consisting entirely of servants' rooms and service areas – kitchen, servants' hall, etc.

The gothic houses built in the early nineteenth century were frequently in a rather restrained style and Donthorne's Cromer Hall, first constructed in the 1820s but rebuilt after a fire of 1829, is typical. Here the west front is basically symmetrical, but the east is more irregular. Both are constructed of flint and dominated by battlements, turrets, buttresses and pointed windows in a loosely Perpendicular style. A larger and more striking house was Hillington Hall in west Norfolk. Unlike Cromer, which was built from scratch, Donthorne's work here involved extending and remodelling an existing building. The hall was originally built in the 1620s for Richard Hovell but had been altered and extended in the 1760s by William Ffolkes; a large number of drawings and plans for these changes survive in Norfolk Record Office. Donthorne's more extensive alterations were carried out for Sir William J. Ffolkes between 1824 and 1827. The building displayed a number of touches typical of the architect (and to some extent of the period): the rather precise structure of the elevation, symmetrical and almost classical in feeling yet gothic in style; and the use of both traditional local, and modern, materials – local carrstone for the walls, but quoins, pediments and battlements of brick, cemented over (91). The north front was

91. Hillington Hall, Donthorne's elaborate gothic mansion before it was largely demolished in 1946.

92. The site of Hillington Hall from the air: dry conditions reveal a complex palimpsest of parchmarks in the lawn. It is possible to identify the walls of the original seventeenth-century mansion built by Richard Hovell, the extensions made in the 1760s, and the more substantial additions made by Donthorne in the 1820s.

dominated by a great central tower, similar to those erected by Donthorne's mentor Jeffry Wyattville at Ashridge in Hertfordshire and elsewhere. Soaring towers had been entirely absent from the Palladian style of the previous period: they were now a common feature of country houses of whatever style.

At the same time as the house was being remodelled, there were numerous alterations to its surroundings, many intended to complement its new architecture. The old south-eastern entrance was replaced by two drives, approaching the house from the south-west and north-east, and where these met the public road, gothic lodges with tall arches and towers were erected – again to designs by Donthorne. The home farm and stables were also given a modish gothic veneer, and the new drive was carried over the Babingley river by an impressive bridge, complete with a plaque carrying the Ffolkes family's heraldic device, the fleur-de-lys. The hall was almost entirely demolished in 1946 – only its eastern wing being retained – but aerial photographs dramatically reveal its ground plan (92). What we see is, in fact, a complex palimpsest: some of the walls appearing as parchmarks relate to the original seventeenth-century house, others to the alterations of the eighteenth century, most to the additions made by Donthorne.

A TASTE FOR HISTORY

Donthorne, of course, was not the only architect designing gothic houses in this period. In the 1840s, Sir John Jacob Buxton commissioned the architect Edward Blore to alter and extend Shadwell Lodge, a house originally built by the gentleman architect John Buxton in the 1720s but extended by John Soane in 1789. Blore's alterations were fairly limited in scale and in a rather restrained gothic style. Buxton's son, Sir Robert, wanted something grander and commissioned S.S. Teulon to extend it further: the building work was carried out between 1857 and 1866. The result was a massive yet intricately detailed, determinedly asymmetrical gothic pile, a medievalist fantasy with turrets and towers and even a cavernous open hall with a beamed roof. It had no fewer than fifty-two rooms (93). The architect employed a range of materials – flint, brick,

93. Shadwell Park – this elaborate gothic house was largely the work S.S. Teulon, who altered and extended an existing gothic house between 1857 and 1866.

94. Costessey Hall, a late sixteenth-century house, was massively extended as an elaborate gothic pile by the architect J.C. Buckler in the 1830s, '40s and '50s. The chapel, just visible to the left of the photograph, was an earlier addition of c. 1800 – the owners, the Jerninghams, were Roman Catholics. Buckler's design was dominated by a great castellated tower.

and carrstone – in a number of different combinations. The house's name was altered to fit its new appearance and status, from Shadwell Lodge to Shadwell Park. As at Hillington, the grounds were also altered at this time. A suitably dramatic approach from the west was created along a sweeping drive running through the parkland. The construction of this great house may well have stretched the resources of the Buxtons, who were not a tremendously wealthy family. In 1898, as the agricultural depression deepened, they were forced to sell to the Musker family, who employed the architect H.J. Green to make further alterations to the house two years later. The house as it stands, however, remains largely the work of Teulon.

Shadwell was one of several houses in the county built in the mid-nineteenth century in a wild, romantic gothic style. Costessey Hall is another example. This was a vast building, although one that has left few traces. Here again an important architect – J.C. Buckler – massively expanded an existing house. The late sixteenth-century E-plan manor house of the Jerningham family had already been extended around 1800 by Edward Jerningham, with the addition of a gothic chapel (the Jerninghams were Roman Catholics). In the 1820s a decision was made to build

something altogether bigger. The original intention, it is said, was to completely demolish the old hall but this was not done, due to the intervention of the Prince of Wales, and as a result the great mass of Buckler's red-brick Tudor and Gothic pile reared above it, dwarfing it entirely (94). It was a rich fantasy, crenellated, pinnacled and dominated by a great tower. It was set in an equally vast park, and approached by several drives with elaborate gothic lodges at their entrances. Some of these remain, but the hall itself was largely demolished in the 1920s and only the ivy-clad ruins of the tower now survive, marooned, somewhat incongruously, in the middle of a golf course (95).

Shadwell and Costessey were somewhat exceptional. Most Victorian gentlemen preferred something less extravagant and most gothic country houses were more Jacobean or Elizabethan than medieval in appearance: less imposing, more manor house than castle. Stow Bardolph, designed in the early 1870s by David Brandon, is a good example (96 and 97). According to the journal *The Builder*,

The walls throughout are constructed of local bricks, faced with deep coloured red bricks from the adjoining county of Suffolk. The cornices, quoin

95. Costessey Hall was demolished in the 1920s and only the ivy-clad ruins of its tower now survive, marooned, somewhat incongruously, in the middle of Costessey golf course.

96. *Stow Bardolph Hall, designed in the early 1870s by David Brandon, is a good illustration of the more homely, 'manorial' form of gothic that was popular among the Norfolk gentry in the second half of the nineteenth century. (From an illustration in the magazine* The Builder*)*

97. *Stow Bardolph Hall, photographed shortly before demolition in 1994. The building had been derelict and unoccupied for many years.*

stones, the plinths, string courses, and dressings round the doors and windows are executed in Little Casterton freestone from the quarries near Stamford, in the county of Northampton, and the roofs are covered with green Bangor slates.

Many landowners opted for a style firmly based on the kind of compact brick residences erected in the late sixteenth century at Heydon or Barningham, featuring finials and angle pilasters and mullion windows – like Dunston Hall to the south of Norwich, designed in 1859 by J.C. Buckler (98). A few adopted a style derived from that of Jacobean Renaissance house – that is, they followed the example of buildings like Blickling Hall. Lynford Hall, built between 1856 and 1861 to designs by William Burn, reflects this influence. Here the battlements and turrets of medieval gothic are replaced by lead cupolas and shaped gables. Similar in many ways was Sandringham, built for the Prince of Wales in the 1870s. Yet another antiquarian alternative was to employ a style based on the late Elizabethan Renaissance, as exemplified in great houses like Wollaton Hall in Nottinghamshire or Longleat in Wiltshire. This was used for the magnificent house – now a magnificent ruin – erected in the 1840s at Bylaugh, which was designed for the Lombe family by Charles Barry.

Various theories have been advanced as to why these ancient but indigenous styles of architecture came into fashion in this period, especially for country houses. At one level the trend was – like the rediscovery of Greek architecture which encouraged the Greek Revival style – a symptom of the growing interest in archaeology: it is no coincidence that the Norfolk Archaeological Society was founded in 1845. But it has also been suggested that the trend had more deep-seated causes. In a rapidly changing world, it may have reflected a hankering after a supposedly more stable, harmonious and paternalistic past, before the upheavals of the industrial and agricultural revolutions, and the attendant threats and uncertainties that these brought. The owner of a house like Stow Bardolph could pose as – perhaps convince himself that he was in truth – a paternalistic squire, looking after the needs of a community of contented yeomen, rather than the monopoly landowner in a polarised society dominated by large tenant farms, inhabited by impoverished landless labourers and threatened by an increasingly vociferous urban middle class. There may be some truth in all this: although to some extent, in the increasingly commercialised world of nineteenth-century Britain, fashions changed simply because fashions changed. Something new was always required to satisfy the demand for novelty, and classically derived designs had held sway now for more than a century.

Yet there was one great advantage that gothic and Jacobean, and to some extent the other new styles of the nineteenth century, had over the previous classical mode. They allowed – indeed, encouraged – the development of more asymmetrical, sprawling plans. This in turn permitted the further proliferation of entertaining and reception rooms which had begun in the previous century. To the existing repertoire of library, drawing room and dining room were now added morning rooms, billiard rooms, even smoking rooms. At the same time the number of bedrooms tended to increase, for this was the great age of the country house party: encouraged by improvements in road travel and the spread of the rail network, landowners entertained on a lavish scale. Guests would expect to be put up – in suitable comfort – for several days, as they indulged in game shooting and in a variety of less structured recreational activities. More household servants were, of course, needed for this kind of thing and they too had to be accommodated, putting still further demands on space, especially as the internal layout of the country house was increasingly zoned on class lines: that is, every care was taken to keep the servants and all their activities carefully segregated from the family and polite visitors. Long

98. Dunston Hall to the south of Norwich, designed in 1859 by J.C. Buckler for Robert Kellett Long. (Photographed in 1990)

rambling wings allowed this to be achieved with relative ease, and with the development of the bell-pull servants could be summoned from a distance whenever they were required. Moreover, in an increasingly moral climate, it was felt that male and female servants should be kept as far apart as possible, their accommodation (and where possible their places of work) kept spatially distinct. This segregation was mirrored, to some extent, in the increasing division of the 'polite' space of the house into male and female spheres. Thus the dining room and boudoir were considered female spaces, the smoking room and billiard room essentially male ones, and at certain times of the day (especially after the evening meal) the different sexes would separate. All this further encouraged the extension and complication of house plans.

PARTERRES AND PARKLANDS

As well as witnessing radical changes in the style and planning of country houses, the nineteenth century also saw important changes in their setting. Important residences continued to be surrounded by parks, but there were significant developments in the way that these were arranged and planted. More importantly, the nineteenth century saw the return to prominence of gardens and pleasure grounds. Towards the end of the eighteenth century a number of writers had criticised the rather stereotyped simplicity of the landscape style of Brown and his 'imitators'. 'Picturesque' writers like Richard Payne Knight and Uvedale Price, and working designers like Repton began to advocate more varied and lush planting within the park, the introduction of more ruggedness and variety into Brown's rather bland landscapes, and the reintroduction of structure and order in front of the mansion in the form of terraces or even formal gardens. In the course of the nineteenth century, such ideas gradually came to be widely shared, in Norfolk as elsewhere.

Two of the most famous 'picturesque' designers worked in Norfolk. John Claudius Loudon – who described himself in 1805 as the first landscape designer 'professing to follow Mr Price's principles' – prepared designs for Stradsett (1810) and Gillingham (1812): William Sawrey Gilpin worked at Wolterton and Gunton in the 1820s and at Keswick in the late 1830s. Wolterton perhaps shows most clearly the true character of 'picturesque' landscape design. George Stanley Repton (Humphry's youngest son) had recently completed extensive modifications to Wolterton Hall, which included the construction of an elaborate balcony at first-floor level on the south front, from which open stairs led down to the gardens. Gilpin's work was closely related to these alterations. In the area immediately below the balcony he created elaborate parterres of shaped beds containing a variety of bulbs and bedding plants (crocuses, geraniums, primroses, and anemones: 'as much colour as can be got', as Gilpin put it). To the south, away from the hall, these were bounded by a substantial east–west terrace, ornamented with urns. This still survives, a wide feature that provided a suitable place to promenade and to enjoy views over the parkland beyond (99). The terrace – typically for Gilpin – is ranged asymmetrically in relation to the house, extending further to the west than to the east. (The almost identical terrace which he designed for Keswick in 1837 does the same.) From each end, steps led down to paths that meandered through extensive areas of shrubbery.

Gilpin also gave more variety to the parkland to the south. In the area between the terrace and the northern shore of the lake the smooth parkland turf was broken up by islands of shrubbery, planted with a mixture of evergreens (cedar, silver fir) and deciduous shrubs (such as lilac). The shores of the lake were made more irregular, an island created and the planting around made more lush and varied. It is

99. Design for the garden, terrace and park at Wolterton by William Sawrey Gilpin, undated, c. 1828. (Wolterton Hall archives)

important to emphasise, however, that all this was not simply intended to provide a single static view from the house or the terrace. Like other landscapes in the 'picturesque' mode, the complexity and detail were there to be explored, and Gilpin contrived a series of carefully designed views from the circuit path laid out around the shore of the lake.

The trends – towards more varied planting in parks and more elaborate, formal gardens across the main façades of houses – intensified as the century progressed. At the greatest houses, terraces became increasingly prominent and more 'Italianate' in their details, with a plethora of vases, pedestals and fountains. The famous designer William Andrews Nesfield, often working in association with the country house architect William Burn, was the main mover here. Nesfield's hallmark was the wide balustraded terrace on which extensive geometric parterres were displayed, their designs based (although much more loosely than he himself claimed) on genuine seventeenth-century models. In Norfolk, Burn and Nesfield worked together on two main commissions. At Holkham a huge terrace was constructed in the 1850s, all along the south front of the hall. Upon it Nesfield laid out elaborate parterres, defined by low box hedges, which still survive today although in slightly modified form (54). There were straight gravel paths, numerous short flight of stairs and a central pool with a statue of Perseus and Andromeda by C.R. Smith, which had formerly been displayed at the Great Exhibition of 1851. From the main terrace a narrower extension to the east led to the conservatory, designed by Burn in a vaguely classical style. Equally striking are the gardens laid out at Lynford when the hall was rebuilt by Burn. Nesfield also designed the gardens at Bylaugh (only traces now remain); at Honingham; and there is some evidence that he was involved in laying out the extensive terraces at Hillington in the 1850s, although by this time there were plenty of firms and designers eager to provide similar settings for the country house. Substantial balustraded terraces were prominently placed across the main façades at Merton in the 1840s; at Melton Constable and Westwick in the 1850s (100); at Taverham in 1858–9; at Buckenham Tofts in the 1860s (now surviving only in earthwork form); at Stow Bardolph in 1873; and at Letton in 1882.

The reintroduction of formal structure beside the mansion did not invariably take the form of Italianate terraces. At Houghton, for example, the late nineteenth century saw the creation of a complex parterre, composed of gravel paths and beds dug deep into the subsoil on the level ground to the west of the hall. This has long since been swept away, with the exception of a number of small clumps of box that now stand, somewhat incongruously, in what is now an area of featureless lawn: but the pattern of paths and beds is still visible in the summer, especially from the air (101).

Small specialised gardens, often devoted to a particular kind of plant or a particular 'theme', also proliferated in the course of the century. Shrubberies grew more extensive, threaded with paths bordered with box, yew, laurel and rhododendron. Arboreta – tree collections – also became popular, although few survive in good condition in the county. (However, interesting remains do exist at Ryston and Langley: picture 57.) Exotic trees were also increasingly planted in the open parkland, notably the monkey puzzle (introduced in 1795), as at Barningham and Hunstanton; and the Wellingtonia (1852), with notable examples at Catton, Raynham, Heacham and Lynford. At the latter site, as at Dunston, these outlandish

100. Westwick Hall stands within fine terraced gardens, constructed in the 1860s.

101. *Dry conditions reveal this astonishing parchmark in the lawn immediately to the west of Houghton Hall – an elaborate parterre of the mid-nineteenth century. The dark areas represent flower beds, cut deeply into the subsoil.*

trees were used for avenues – another geometric feature that now experienced something of a revival.

There were probably several reasons why gardens, and especially geometric gardens, enjoyed renewed popularity in this period. In part it was because consumers wanted something new, had grown bored with the fashions of the previous century with their emphasis on open parkland. But in part the change was associated with the new styles of architecture, for terraces and parterres made a particularly suitable setting for houses in gothic or Elizabethan style. A growing enthusiasm for horticulture, encouraged by the availability of new exotic varieties through Britain's far-flung trading links, was also important. A variety of new half-hardy plants, especially pelargoniums, were 'bedded out' in lavish geometric displays. Lastly, it is possible that the growing cultural dominance of the middle classes (who had always maintained fairly structured gardens, even in the eighteenth century) was a significant factor, for this was an age of increasing upward mobility and many nineteenth-century country house owners had relatively humble origins.

Whatever the explanation, gardens of all kinds increased in sophistication and scale, and this included kitchen gardens. Generally speaking, their overall plan tended to become simpler and more standardised after the wave of late eighteenth-century experimentation (although some complex, polygonal layouts were attempted, as at Bylaugh and Didlington in the 1850s). But their internal features grew steadily more sophisticated. Glasshouses proliferated as improved technology (and changes in the tax on glass) allowed mass production. By the 1870s most kitchen gardens could boast an elaborate array of glass, much of it made by the Norwich firm of Boulton & Paul, although some examples were brought from much further afield: the firm of Messengers, at Loughborough, for example, supplied many of the glasshouses for the gardens at Melton Constable Hall. Glasshouses were usually ranged along the south side of the north wall of the garden, where they would be most sheltered and receive the most sunlight: the colder, darker north side was occupied by stores, tool sheds, potting sheds and sometimes bothies where the under-gardeners lived and slept. The majority of glasshouses were lean-to structures with simple sloping roofs, although many forcing houses were full-span and ranged north–south (rather than east–west) in order to provide equal amounts of sunlight throughout the growing area. Other variants included vineries, which were normally provided with high, steeply sloping roofs and low arches in the front wall (the vines were planted in the front of the house and the arches allowed their roots to spread widely outside); cucumber houses, similarly shaped but narrower and considerably lower; and 'pine' houses, in which pineapples were grown in the middle of a low glasshouse with a shallow pitched roof, on a raised level base surrounded by a walkway. The greatest landed estates, such as Holkham, maintained vast arrays of glass (102).

The kitchen garden, even more than in the previous century, was an aesthetic as well as a utilitarian area, and was usually connected to the gravel walks threading the shrubberies and pleasure grounds. The neat box hedges flanking the paths, the central dipping pond, the carefully espaliered fruit trees growing against the walls or on iron frames – all exuded an air of efficient production. And the kitchen garden also demonstrated its owners' familiarity with up-to-date gadgets and technologies, including heating systems utilising piped hot water for the greenhouses, which were almost ubiquitous by the 1870s. Yet although kitchen gardens might be places of resort and recreation as well as production, they continued to be located in relatively marginal positions, and indeed there are more truly isolated examples from the Victorian period (including those at Catton, Didlington, Lynford and Merton) than from the eighteenth century.

102. The kitchen garden, Holkham, was constructed on a new site in the 1790s and grew steadily in complexity throughout the following century, with particularly elaborate ranges of glass. The tall structures against the north wall are vine houses. In the foreground, outside the walled enclosure, is the orangery designed in the 1790s by Samuel Wyatt.

BYLAUGH

Three striking examples will perhaps serve to illustrate the Victorian achievement in country house architecture and landscape design. We may begin with Bylaugh, the construction of which had a considerable contemporary impact in Norfolk and beyond. According to tradition, the Bylaugh estate was won from Richard Lloyd in a game of cards by Sir John Lombe of Great Melton in 1796. When the latter died childless in 1817 his estates passed to his brother Edward, together with a considerable sum of money, deposited in trust for the building of a suitable mansion in a prominent position somewhere on the estate. At first Edward Lombe did nothing about the bequest, but in 1828 William Wilkins the younger was commissioned to submit designs for a new house. These, however, were rejected and the house remained unbuilt for another twenty years. Nevertheless, towards the end of his life Lombe – who was now living abroad – commissioned the architects Charles Barry Junior and Richardson Banks to prepare a new design. Barry was the son of Sir Charles Barry who had built the Houses of Parliament with A.W. Pugin; Banks had for many years been Chief Assistant in the elder Barry's office.

The house was vast and – built on a virgin site – made a considerable impression. According to the London journal the *Athenaeum* in 1852:

> One of the wonders of the modern world may be seen near East Dereham in Norfolk, in what a few years back was only a turnip field . . . A more comfortable house it would be difficult to imagine: neither Holkham nor Houghton, those Norfolk wonders, can compare with it for either appearance or comfort.

No expense was spared. The house was built of magnesian limestone brought from the Midlands and was one of the first houses to be constructed with the support of steel girders. In style it was Elizabethan, strongly reminiscent of (and presumably partly modelled on) Wollaton in Nottinghamshire. It had angle turrets and an imposing tower (103). The mansion was completed in 1851 and the new owner, Charles Lombe, returned to court to ask for the remaining balance of money to be released. This request was refused by the trustees, however, who insisted that all the available funds should be expended on the property. As a result, a substantial stable block (complete with clock tower) and a wall was constructed, extending for 9 miles around the perimeter of the park.

The park covered no less than 736 acres (298 hectares) and included a large wood (occupying the former site of Bylaugh Heath) as well as numerous smaller clumps

103. Bylaugh Hall as it was in the late nineteenth century. Note the formal parterres, designed by William Andrews Nesfield, in the foreground.

and belts. Bylaugh demonstrates clearly how the appeal of the landscape park remained strong in the Victorian age: but, as we have noted, gardens were making a comeback, and – with no expense to be spared – the grounds here were laid out by William Andrews Nesfield, 'the well-known landscape artist', with complex parterres and balustraded terraces providing fine views across the Wensum valley. Nesfield, in fact, also advised on the precise position of the house, 'a very fine position on a sheltered knoll' with 'a full South exposure', as the sale catalogue of 1917 put it. Bylaugh was a unique creation: nowhere else in Norfolk were a house and park of this magnitude established during Victoria's reign.

The hall was let to various tenants during the first half of the twentieth century, the Lombe family preferring to reside in their more manageable residence at Great Melton, and later at Marlingford. Bylaugh was sold in 1918 and occupied by the Air Ministry during the Second World War, then passed through several more owners before partial demolition in 1950. It now stands, a forlorn but impressive ruin, flanked by the crumbling remains of Nesfield's terraces (104). The park is now entirely under the plough.

104. Bylaugh Hall today: a forlorn and roofless ruin, its garden overgrown and its parkland ploughed.

105. *Lynford Hall, designed by the architect William Burn and built in the 1850s, but reduced in size after a fire in 1928. The terraced gardens are by William Andrews Nesfield.*

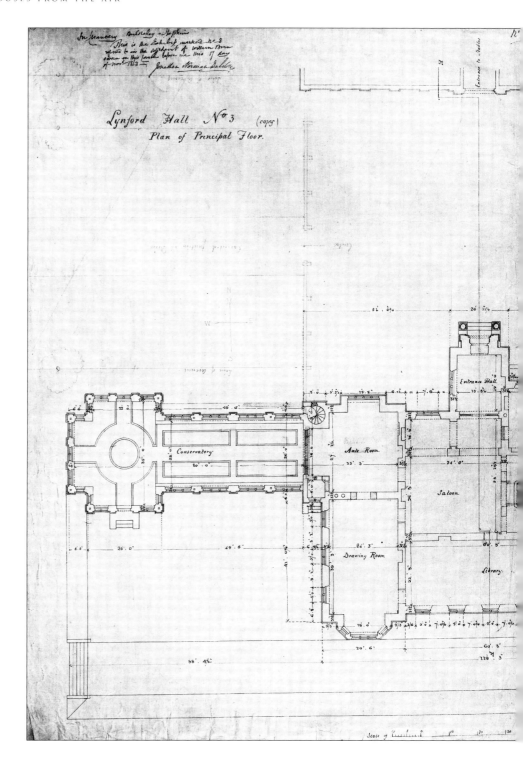

LYNFORD

Lynford Hall, unlike Bylaugh, had a long and complex history before the Victorian age. There have, in comparatively recent times, been three different Lynford Halls on three different sites. The first, built *c.* 1500, was abandoned by James Nelthorpe in 1717 in favour of a new house a little distance to the north. A later owner, Sir Richard Sutton, commissioned Charles Robert Cockerell to alter and remodel the

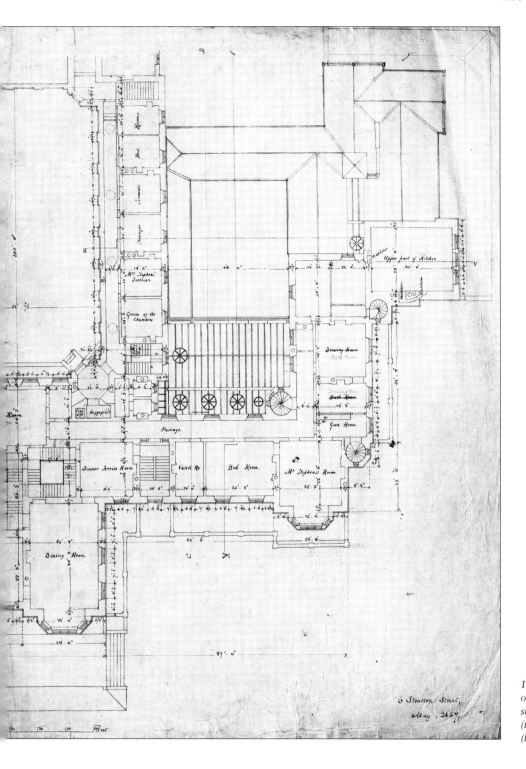

106. Lynford Hall: Burn's original plans for the house, showing the lost western range (to the right) and orangery (left).

house in 1827. According to a note in the West Tofts parish register in 1859, there were other alterations, for the house had 'been greatly added to at various times, the whole of which additions were most ingeniously concealed by an outer coating of white brick'. This note was entered in the register because the house was in the process of being demolished. The site had been acquired by the wealthy S. Lyne Stephens, who commissioned the architect William Burn to design a new house. This was on a new site, some 450 metres to the north: the old hall was demolished, although not very thoroughly, so that the ruins of the cellars, fragments of walling and the remains of the early nineteenth-century gardens still survive within the undergrowth of a Forestry Commission plantation.

Bylaugh was an exercise in English Renaissance revival; Lynford in contrast was an attempt to copy the more domestic Jacobean style of Blickling and its like (105). It was built of red brick with stone dressings and has prominent shaped gables and turrets with lead cupolas. As Burn's plan reveals (106), it was a rambling edifice, carefully designed to ensure maximum segregation of servants and served, and – especially among the former group – male and female. The house still survives, although following a fire in the 1920s it was extensively rebuilt, and the west range demolished. Here, too, Nesfield laid out the gardens. The *Gardeners Chronicle* described them as Nesfield's 'largest and best'. They were bounded by low balustrades 'with the usual coping for vases', and featured 'the customary terraces with sloping banks of turf, geometrical designs of Box and flower beds, borders with walks of smashed bricks etc'. The beds were 'well furnished with flowering and foliage plants of the usual character'. As at Holkham the centrepiece was a large statue: 'a magnificent mistake – two bulls in mortal combat – which might with great propriety be removed to the forecourt of the mansion'. This latter change was subsequently effected, but the basic framework of 'hard landscaping' otherwise remains as Nesfield designed it, although the original planting has – with exception of a number of large yews – largely disappeared. (The gardens were abandoned and neglected for many years, and only restored in the 1970s.) The park was expanded to the north, and by the 1880s covered an area of more than 100 hectares, much of it occupied by woodland. To the west of the house a fine avenue of Wellingtonias was planted – one of the finest pieces of nineteenth-century planting in the county. This still survives in reasonable condition, but much of the surrounding landscape has been engulfed in Forestry Commission plantations.

SANDRINGHAM

The construction of large country houses began to tail off in the 1870s, but Sandringham stands as a magnificent exception. This was almost, but not quite, an entirely new building. Some time around 1820 Henry Hoste Henley demolished most of the old Sandringham Hall and erected a new, rather low house with side wings. Following his death the estate, comprising some 7,000 acres, passed eventually to Charles Spencer Cowper, who commissioned S.S. Teulon to add a conservatory (later used as a billiard room). In 1861 the estate was purchased by Edward, Prince of Wales (later Edward VII) for £220,000. He soon began to make improvements and modifications to the house, and in 1870 began to rebuild on a massive scale, retaining only the Teulon conservatory. The architect was A.J. Humbert – not a very well-known designer, but a favourite of the royal family, who had employed him on a number of earlier commissions, including the Royal Mausoleum at Frogmore and Whippingham Church near Osborne on the Isle of Wight.

The new house – like Lynford – was built in a broadly Jacobean style, of red brick with Ketton stone dressings, and had numerous gables and two striking cupolas – one of them surmounting a turret on the eastern façade (107). In 1883 a ballroom designed by R.W. Ellis was added, projecting eastwards from the southern end of the east façade, in a rather more flamboyant Jacobean style and built in part of the local carrstone; and in 1891 – following a serious fire – there were further additions and alterations, and a second storey was added to the north-eastern end. The house was equipped with all the latest technology: water was supplied from an elaborate water-tower built in the 1880s a mile to the south-east – a red brick structure with an Italianate turret. The Prince also modified the grounds (there had been a park here since the eighteenth century), and here too the triumphs of modern technology were apparent. The large and elaborate wrought- and cast-iron gates at the Norwich road entrance were designed by Thomas

107. Sandringham was purchased by Edward, Prince of Wales in 1861, and the house rebuilt on a grand scale during the 1870s by the architect A.J. Humbert. The fine formal gardens to the north, with geometrical pattern of box-edged beds and flanking avenue of pleached limes, are a twentieth-century addition designed by G.A. Jellicoe.

Jekyll and made by the Norwich firm of Barnard, Bishop & Barnard: they were shown at the Great Exhibition of 1862 and given by the County of Norfolk – that is, by the principal county landowners – to the Prince the following year as a wedding present. The drive, like the interior of the house, was illuminated by gaslight. The kitchen gardens, which are located across the public road and thus well outside the park, were extensive and provided with magnificent ranges of glasshouses.

The pleasure grounds around the house extend to over 12 hectares and contain two lakes, created by the landscape designer W.B. Thomas in the 1870s, in part by adapting a smaller, earlier lake created for the previous house. On the north shore of the upper lake there is a good example of 'Pulhamite' artificial rockwork, forming a large rockery and a boathouse/grotto. The fine trees growing within the pleasure grounds include some (mainly oaks) retained from the eighteenth-century park, and much planting from the 1860s and '70s. The gardens in the immediate area of the house were laid out in the customary formal style, but have subsequently been much altered and simplified. In particular, the west flower garden was replaced with lawns in 1947 (although the terrace from which this was viewed still survives). At the same time the north garden, with its geometrical pattern of box-edged beds and flanking avenue of pleached limes, was designed by G.A. Jellicoe.

Like earlier houses and their landscapes, those of the nineteenth century were very much a product of their time. This was an age of empire, commerce, industry and technology: and the country house reveals the ambivalence of landowners to the new order. On the one hand, modernity was celebrated – new technologies were embraced in the form of innovative building materials and various domestic comforts. On the other, it was shunned, as architects and garden designers drew on the remote past for inspiration.

POSTSCRIPT

Although various forms of non-agricultural income – from investment in trade and industry, from the spoils of government office – had always been a significant factor in the finances of Norfolk's landowners, most relied heavily on their agricultural rents. In the late 1870s, however, a serious depression, caused mainly by competition from imports from the New World, set in: a depression that was particularly serious in arable farming areas like Norfolk. At the same time, changes in political structures in Britain, at both a local and national level – the gradual extension of suffrage, the development of local government – ensured that the landed rich no longer dominated local life in quite the way that they had done. As a consequence of these and other developments, large houses and extensive landscapes of fashionable display gradually lost their significance during the late nineteenth and early twentieth centuries.

New country houses were still sporadically constructed or extensively remodelled. One example is Riddlesworth Hall, overlooking the River Waveney in south-west Norfolk. Following a disastrous fire in 1899 the owners, the Champion family, commissioned the Norwich architect H.J. Green to design a new house: an unusual structure, classical in style and with a central pediment supported by Corinthian columns, yet asymmetrical in layout. Another is Pickenham Hall, where Donthorne's Neoclassical house was extensively remodelled in a vaguely Georgian style by the architect R.W. Weir Schultz, and fine gardens laid out in the fashionable 'arts and crafts' style, with a terrace of stone and brick, yew hedges, a sunken garden and a Chinese garden. More dramatic is Sennowe Hall, where the original eighteenth-century mansion was extensively remodelled and massively extended by Norwich architect George Skipper around 1906. The resulting pile (108) has a main façade of seventeen bays. The gardens laid out to the south matched the Italianate architecture of the hall itself, with terracing on three levels and numerous statues, many by Italian craftsmen.

Where houses were rebuilt in this way, however, it was generally a sign that the owners had access to large amounts of income other than agricultural rents, or were new recruits to the landed class from the world of commerce or industry: Sennowe, for example, had been acquired in 1898 by Thomas Cook, grandson of the founder of the famous travel firm. But by the early years of the twentieth century most successful businessmen, while they might desire a home in the country, were less keen on acquiring an extensive landed estate, with all the problems and burdens this might bring. A house in the country, rather than a country house, was what many now wanted, including many established landed families; and preferably it should be in a healthy coastal location. Houses of moderate size built in 'arts and crafts' style using mixtures of local and modern materials were increasingly popular. Happisburgh Manor, overlooking the North Sea in the north-east of the county, is a good example: designed in 1900 by the architect Detmar Blow for the Cator family, it is constructed of a mixture of thin tiles, flint, brick and pebbles, and consists of an oblong block with wings extending diagonally to give a plan like a butterfly. More extravagant is Home Place at Holt (originally called Voewood), designed for the Revd Percy Lloyd by E.S. Prior in 1903–5. It cost £60,000 to build, with its

108. *Sennowe Hall: the original eighteenth-century house was greatly extended in 1906–8 to designs by the Norwich architect George Skipper and provided with elaborate Italianate terraced gardens.*

109. The site of West Tofts Hall, demolished in the 1950s following its incorporation into the Breckland Battle Training Area.

walls of concrete faced with pebbles and larger stones, its elevation a riot of columns, gables and parapets in a range of local materials. Like other houses of this period, Home Place is like a traditional vernacular house seen through a distorting mirror.

Expensive houses might thus still be erected, but – with exceptions like Riddlesworth or Sennowe – these were no longer country houses in the usual sense of the word. For the most part, existing estates went gradually downhill, their mansions, parks and surrounding land sliding slowly into dereliction. Robert Ketton, owner of the Felbrigg estate, later described how, between 1872 and 1924:

Repairs were neglected, to farmhouse and farm buildings and cottages alike. Land was undrained, watercourses became choked, nothing was done to drives and roads . . . Damp began to soak everywhere through the roofs. The shrubbery grew into an entanglement and the lawn into a hayfield.

Agricultural fortunes revived briefly during the First World War, but the depression deepened again in the inter-war years. Many estates changed hands, others were broken up, especially those of the local gentry who had, by and large, fewer alternative resources on which to fall back than the largest landowners. Sales had begun gradually in the 1880s and '90s, increased steadily in number during the early 1900s, but became a deluge in the immediate post-war years. Between 1918 and 1921 no fewer than fourteen Norfolk estates of 800 hectares or more were put on the market. Estates located in the more agriculturally marginal areas of the county were especially vulnerable to economic decline. Many were purchased by the Forestry Commission during the 1920s, the acquisition reports drawn up prior to purchase painting a picture of unrelieved gloom. That for Croxton Park, for example, made in 1929, described the estate as 'partly heath and partly low grade light arable or pasture land which has passed, or is about to pass, out of cultivation'.

During the Second World War many country houses and their parks were requisitioned by the army, and their fabric often suffered serious deterioration. In the post-war period agricultural fortunes revived but landowners were badly

110. The country house as archaeological site: the parchmarks of Honingham Hall, demolished in 1967. The parchmarks reveal the outline of a house built in the seventeenth century (but incorporating an earlier building), extended and remodelled in the 1770s and 1850s.

affected both by a general economic recession and by the fact that government policy ensured that rents rose less rapidly than farm profits. In addition, death duties under the Labour administration rose to 75 per cent, while maintenance costs soared as wage levels rose. Estates continued to come on the market: Riddlesworth in 1946, Ketteringham in 1947, Garboldisham in 1948. Only in the late 1950s did the fortunes of large landowners begin to improve, as land prices and rents rose again, and as landowners took more and more of their estates back in hand, farming on their own account in an increasingly profitable climate.

What has been the impact on the landscape of these momentous changes? Numerous country houses survive in Norfolk, a surprising number still occupied by the families who owned them during the nineteenth century. Indeed, a substantial minority are still in the hands of the families who built them in the eighteenth century. But many disappeared in the course of the twentieth century. A number were pulled down in the inter-war years – North Elmham and Weston Longville were demolished in the 1920s, Costessey reduced to a ruin in the 1930s. But it was in the immediate aftermath of the Second World War that demolitions came thick and fast. Gawdy, Heacham, Hillington and Great Melton were all levelled in the 1940s, Morton Hall was largely pulled down in 1952, Buckenham Tofts and West Tofts (109) in the 1950s, following their incorporation into the Breckland Battle Training Area, Honingham Hall went in 1967. Stow Bardolph was knocked down in 1995 after many years of dereliction, its owners residing in a converted stable block.

Many of these places have themselves become archaeological sites. Some survive as ruins: Costessey, the remains of its tall tower marooned within a golf course on the outskirts of Norwich; Great Melton, its walls surviving almost to first-floor level but choked with vegetation. Others are now visible only from the air, as networks of parch-marks – like Honingham (110) or Weston Longville, which now lies on land converted first to a dinosaur theme park, subsequently to a golf course (111).

At both Great Melton and Gawdy the park survives largely intact even though the house has gone. Indeed, in general parks have survived surprisingly well – better than the gardens attached to great mansions which, under pressure from declining resources and escalating wage bills, usually underwent gradual simplification in the early and middle decades of the twentieth century. True, most parks experienced much loss of timber in this period, and their woods suffered from poor management. But in most cases at least a part of the parkland turf survived unploughed. During the last two decades, in a new climate of enthusiasm for 'heritage', large areas of former parkland have been returned to grass, as at Wolterton or Houghton, with or without the financial incentives provided by such schemes as 'Countryside Stewardship', and large amounts of tree-planting have taken place.

Where country houses have escaped demolition they have not always remained as private houses. Some, like Gunton Hall, have been saved from dereliction by being converted into a number of up-market apartments. Others have found new uses in the leisure industry, especially those on the outskirts of Norwich. Sprowston Hall is a golf and country club, Dunston a hotel, golf course and restaurant. In the latter case, successive aerial photographs vividly capture the extent of the alterations to the landscape consequent on this change of use (98 and 112).

Several of the country houses, or their grounds, discussed and illustrated in this volume are open to the public on a regular or frequent basis. Some of these, like Oxburgh, Felbrigg, Blickling and Sheringham, are in the hands of the National Trust; others, like Holkham or Houghton, are still in private ownership. The perennial interest in this aspect of 'our' heritage which the popularity of these

111. *The country house as archaeological site: parchmarks reveal the plan of Weston Longville Hall, built in the late 1770s and demolished in 1926, in front of the surviving stable block.*

112. New roles for old houses: Dunston Hall, now a golf club and country house hotel (compare picture 98).

places attests – and of which this small volume is yet another manifestation – is perhaps symptomatic of an age of uncertainty, as Britain faces its post-colonial, post-industrial future. Whether we regard them as relics of past inequality and oppression, or as symbols of a lost age of wealth and taste, country houses and their parks and gardens continue to make an important impact on the Norfolk landscape, demanding the attention of art historians, archaeologists and historians.

LIST OF AERIAL PHOTOGRAPHS

All the aerial photography in this publication has been taken by Derek Edwards and is the copyright of Norfolk Museums Service, Union House, Gressenhall, East Dereham, Norfolk, NR20 4DR, excepting picture 70, also taken by Derek Edwards, which is copyright of Aerial Archaeology Publications, Lansdown House, Breton Close, Toftwood, East Dereham, Norfolk, NR19 1JH.

Front of dust jacket
   Oxburgh Hall, Oxborough
   (from west) TF7401/ABT/HPW11, 11 July 1997
Back of dust jacket
   (upper) Piper Cub Aircraft G-BLLN, over Houghton
   Hall Kitchen Gardens and Stables, Houghton
   (from west) TF7828/Q/HPZ9, 22 July 1997
   (lower) Holkham Hall, Holkham
   (from south-east) TF8842/AF/DDG14, 10 July 1986
Inside back of dust jacket
   Houghton Hall and Park, Houghton
   (from west) TF7928/ADQ/HPZ4, 22 July 1997
Un-numbered on Half-Title page
   East Barsham Manor, Barsham
   (from south-east) TF9133/M/HPP13, 26 August 1997
Frontispiece
   Blickling Hall and gardens, with areas of lush growth in
      the parched lawns revealing the pattern of tiny
      ornamental flower beds laid out by the Marchioness
      of Lothian in 1872
   (a near vertical view) TG1728/G/AGU7, 3 August 1976
1. Weasenham Hall, Weasenham All Saints
   (from south-west) TF8421/B/AVK13, 17 April 1984
2. Old Warham Hall, Warham
   (a near vertical view) TF9441/K/GHV9, 19 September
   1991
3. Elsing Hall, Elsing
   (from south) TG0316/S/ASF12, 30 March 1983
4. Mannington Hall, Itteringham
   (from south-east) TG1432/C/ASN12, 15 April 1983
5. The site of Buxton Manor, Buxton with Lammas
   (a near vertical view) TG2433/E/GBM6, 28 June 1990
6. Caister Castle, West Caister
   (from south-west) TG5012/S/ATQ21, 29 July 1983
7. Baconsthorpe Castle, Baconsthorpe
   (from west) TG1238/Q/ASJ27, 30 March 1983
8. Middleton Towers, Middleton
   (from south) TF6617/AP/DBF17, 15 July 1986
9. Oxburgh Hall, Oxborough
   (from south-west) TF7401/AB/AZC18, 23 July 1985

11. Hunstanton Hall, Old Hunstanton
   (from south-west) TF6941/M/AYY21, 10 July 1985
12. Hales Hall, Loddon
   (from south-east) TM3696/AA/AXW10, 31 July 1996
14. The moated earthwork site of Wodehouses' Tower,
      Kimberley
   (from north) TG0704/L/ATU9, 5 February 1984
16. East Barsham Manor, Barsham
   (from south-east) TF9133/M/HPP13, 26 August 1997
17. Blickling Hall, Blickling
   (from south) TG1728/ABJ/DLE2, 29 June 1989
18. Heydon Hall, Heydon
   (from south-west) TG1127/P/ASM29, 15 April 1983
19. Barningham Hall, Matlask
   (from west) TG1435/K/DBM15, 16 July 1987
20. Raynham Hall, Raynham
   (from north-east) TF8825/ABA/HGQ23, 12 July 1994
23. Garden earthworks, Oxburgh Hall, Oxborough
   (from north-west) TF7401/AZ/DXJ1, 23 February
   1989
24. Intwood Hall, Keswick
   (from south) TG1904/C/AWW16, 27 April 1984
27. Stiffkey Hall, Stiffkey
   (from south) TF9742/J/AZA14, 10 July 1985
29. Silfield Park, Wymondham
   (from north-east) TM1198/A/ATT3, 5 February 1984
32. Parchmarks of the site of Rougham Hall, Rougham
   (from south-west) TF8220/AR/DJV2, 26 June 1989
36. Melton Constable Hall, Melton Constable
   (from south-west) TG0331/S/AUX18, 4 April 1984
40. Ditchingham Hall, Ditchingham
   (from south-east) TM3292/H/HEG8, 27 July 1995
44. Melton Constable Hall and Park, Melton Constable
   (from north) TG0331/AQ/GZB6, 27 July 1994
46. Aylsham Hall, Aylsham
   (from west) TG1827/M/HHH5, 15 August 1995
49. Booton Hall, Booton
   (from south) TG1122/M/DSR9, 20 July 1988
50. Kimberley Hall, Kimberley
   (from north-east) TG0904/Y/GBZ11, 3 July 1990

51. Houghton Hall and parchmarks of parterre garden, Houghton
    (from west) TF7928/ACQ/DKF6, 26 June 1989
54. Holkham Hall, Holkham
    (from south) TF8842/F/ATK21, 28 July 1983
56. Gunton Hall, Hanworth
    (from south) TG2234/K/DBN28, 17 July 1986
57. Langley Hall, Langley with Hardley
    (from south) TG3500/D/DBV4, 17 July 1986
59. Wolterton Hall, Wickmere
    (from south) TG1631/R/DBM13, 16 July 1986
65. Water House, Houghton Hall Park, Houghton
    (from south) TF7829/D/GYZ14, 27 July 1994
67. Houghton Hall, Park and Gardens, Houghton
    (from south-east) TF7828/ABQ/DET2, 7 May 1987
70. Holkham Hall and Park, Holkham
    (from south-west) ref: 110/21, 15 April 1977,
    © **Aerial Archaeology Publications**
72. Holkham Hall, Church and Park, Holkham
    (from north-west) TF8843/B/JAT13, 19 July 1996
74. The Mausoleum, Blickling Hall Park, Blickling
    (from south-east) TG1629/D/GZC7, 27 July 1994
76. The Kitchen Gardens, Raynham Hall, Raynham
    (from south-west) TF8825/L/DHJ15, 20 March 1989
77. High House, Park and Kitchen Gardens, West Acre
    (from west) TF7918/AC/GSF2, 22 July 1993
78. Honing Hall, Honing
    (from south) TG3229/A/HQB18, 26 August 1997
79. Letton Hall, Letton
    (from south-east) TF9705/AE/DAQ1, 30 June 1986
80. Shotesham Hall, Shotesham
    (from west) TM2298/P/HEF29, 27 July 1995
81. Raveningham Hall, Raveningham
    (from south) TM3996/P/DPW9, 21 February 1989
84. Beeston St Lawrence Hall, Ashmanhaugh
    (from north-west) TG3321/H/HEH1, 27 July 1995
86. Beeston St Lawrence Hall and Park, Ashmanhaugh
    (from south-east) TG3321/G/HEG30, 27 July 1995
87. Catton Hall and Park, Old Catton
    (from south-west) TG2311/E/HHQ27, 2 August 1995
88. Sheringham Hall and Park, Upper Sheringham
    (from south-east) TG1342/G/HHK28, 15 August 1995
92. The site of Hillington Hall, Hillington
    (near vertical view) TF7226/T/DKE2, 26 June 1991
93. Shadwell Court, Brettenham
    (from north-east) TL9283/L/HGB3, 13 May 1994
95. Costessey Hall, Costessey
    (from south-west) TG1611/Q/HEE28, 27 July 1995
97. Stow Bardolph Hall, Stow Bardolph
    (from south) TF6305/E/DTE2, 27 July 1988
98. Dunston Hall, Stoke Holy Cross
    (from north-west) TG2202/P/DZP14, 5 April 1990
100. Westwick Hall, Westwick
    (from south-west) TG2826/A/HPK1, 8 April 1997
101. Former parterre garden at Houghton Hall, Houghton
    (a near vertical view) TF7028/AP/MC10, 10 December
    1991
102. Kitchen Gardens, Holkham Hall, Holkham
    (from south-east) TF8742/AZ/HFS22, 19 July 1994
104. Bylaugh Hall, Bylaugh
    (from south-west) TG0318/S/AUW1, 4 April 1984
105. Lynford Hall, Lynford
    (from south-east) TL8294/A/AUM12, 2 April 1984
107. Sandringham House, Sandringham
    (from north-west) TF6928/C/AYY19, 10 July 1985
108. Sennowe Hall, Stibbard
    (from south-east) TF9825/A/AWD15, 26 April 1984
109. The site of West Tofts Hall, Lynford
    (from north-west) TL8392/D/AUM 22, 2 April 1984
110. The site of Honingham Hall, Honingham
    (from south) TG1112/P/HGD7, 3 July 1993
111. The site of Weston Longville Hall, Weston Longville
    (from south) TG1017/A/HZL10, 6 July 1994
112. Dunston Hall, Stoke Holy Cross
    (from south-east) TG2202/AA/HEF14, 27 July 1995

A NOTE ON SOURCES

The following brief notes are intended for those readers wanting to know about the information and evidence on which this book is based, or wishing to learn more about particular houses or their grounds.

Useful general works on Norfolk country houses, their gardens and owners include Basil Cozens-Hardy, 'Some Norfolk Halls', *Norfolk Archaeology* 32 (1960), pages 163–208; N. Virgoe and S. Yaxley, *The Manor House in Norfolk* (Ipswich, 1978); N. Pevsner, *The Buildings of England: North East Norfolk and Norwich* (Harmondsworth, 1962); N. Pevsner, *The Buildings of England: Norfolk South and West* (Harmondsworth, 1962); M.J. Armstrong, *History and Antiquities of the County of Norfolk* (10 volumes, Norwich, 1781); J. Kenworthy-Brown, P. Reid, M. Sayer, and D. Watkins, *Burke's and Savill's Guide to Country Houses: Volume III, East Anglia* (London, 1981); R.W. Ketton-Cremer, *Norfolk Portraits* (London, 1944); R.W. Ketton-Cremer, *Norfolk Assembly* (London, 1957); R.W. Ketton-Cremer, *Felbrigg: the Story of a House* (London, 1962); Anthea Taigel and Tom Williamson (eds), *Gardens in Norfolk 1550–1900* (Norwich, 1990); Tom Williamson, *The Archaeology of the Landscape Park* (Oxford, 1998); Tom Williamson, 'Politeness and Palladianism: Archaeology and the Country House', in S. Margeson, B. Ayers, and S. Heywood (eds), *A Festival of Norfolk Archaeology* (Norwich, 1996), pages 133–46; and James Grigor, *The Eastern Arboretum: or, Register of Remarkable Trees, Seats, Gardens &c. in the County of Norfolk* (London, 1841). For new approaches to the post-medieval archaeology of England see Matthew Johnson, *An Archaeology of Capitalism* (Oxford, 1995).

INTRODUCTION

For the history of large estates in England and their impact on the landscape see: J.V. Beckett, *The Aristocracy in England 1660–1914* (Oxford, 1986); H.A. Clemenson, *English Country Houses and Landed Estates* (London, 1982); L. and J.C.F. Stone, *An Open Elite*; Tom Williamson and Liz Bellamy, *Property and Landscape: a Social History of Landownership and the English Countryside* (London, 1987). For Norfolk landowners see, in particular: James Rosenheim, 'An Examination of Oligarchy: the Gentry of Restoration Norfolk, 1660–1720' (unpublished PhD thesis, University of East Anglia, 1981), from which comes the information about Cyril Wynch (page 48); and Nigel Wright, 'The Gentry and their Houses in Norfolk and Suffolk *c.* 1550–1850' (unpublished PhD thesis, Centre of East Anglian Studies, University of East Anglia, 1991). For Norfolk's landscape regions see David Dymond, *The Norfolk Landscape* (London, 1985), and Tom Williamson, *The Origins of Norfolk* (Manchester, 1993). For a more general discussion of the relationship between farming regions and landowning structures see Joan Thirsk, 'Seventeenth-century Agriculture and Social Change', in *Land, Church and People*, supplement to the *Agricultural History Review* 18 (1970), pages 148–77. The distribution of large landed estates in Norfolk is discussed by Susanna Wade Martins, 'Great Estates in the Nineteenth Century', in Peter Wade Martins (ed.), *An Historical Atlas of Norfolk* (Norwich, 1993). Country houses have been little studied by archaeologists but a good introduction to garden archaeology is provided by Chris Taylor, *The Archaeology of Gardens* (Aylesbury, 1983).

CHAPTER 1: TUDOR AND STUART COUNTRY HOUSES

For a general account of the development of architecture in this period see Mark Girouard, *Life in the English Country House: a Social and Architectural History* (Yale, 1978). For Caister Castle, see H.D. Barnes and W.D. Simpson, 'Caister Castle', *Antiquaries Journal* 32 (1952), pages 25–51. For Oxburgh, see Christopher Hussey, 'Hunstanton Hall', *Country Life* 1926, pages 552–9, 586–95; and Nigel Nicolson, 'Oxburgh Hall', in Boris Ford (ed.), *The Cambridge Guide to the Arts in Britain* Vol. 2 (1998), pages 88–95. For Hunstanton see Nigel Wright, 'Gentry and their Houses'. The 1615 map of Hunstanton is in the Norfolk Record Office, le Strange OA1, M5–6. For late medieval houses in Norfolk see Ivan Ringwood, 'Late Medieval and Early Tudor Country Houses in Norfolk' (unpublished MA dissertation, Centre of East Anglian Studies, University of East Anglia, 1997).

The information about Shelton Hall comes from Francis Blomefield, *An Essay Towards a Topographic History of the County of Norfolk* (continued by C. Parkin: 11 volumes, second edition, London, 1805–10), Vol. V, page 272. The drawing is with the Rye manuscripts in the Norfolk Record Office. The map of Channons Manor is also in the NRO: Accn. Barnes 1.5.1986 Map Tree 4. The development of Blickling Hall is discussed in John Maddison's *Blickling Hall* (London, 1987), and in C. Stanley-Milson and J. Newman, 'Blickling Hall: the Building of a Jacobean Mansion', *Architectural History*,

29 (1986), pages 1–42. Heydon is discussed by John Cornforth, 'Heydon Hall, Norfolk and its Village', *Country Life* 172 (1982), pages 246–9.

There is an extensive literature on Raynham Hall, but see in particular: H.L. Bradfer-Lawrence, 'The Building of Raynham Hall', *Norfolk Archaeology* 23 (1929), pages 93–146; John Harris, 'Raynham Hall, Norfolk', *Archaeological Journal* 118 (1961), pages 180–7; and Linda Campbell, 'Sir Roger Townshend and his Family: Gentry Life in Early Seventeenth-Century Norfolk' (unpublished PhD thesis, Centre of East Anglian Studies, University of East Anglia, 1989).

For a general discussion of the development of gardens in the sixteenth and early seventeenth centuries see Roy Strong, *The Renaissance Garden in England* (London, 1979). For the Norfolk experience, see Anthea Taigel and Tom Williamson, 'Some Early Geometric Gardens in Norfolk', *Journal of Garden History* 11 (1991), 1 and 2. The gardens at Besthorpe, Intwood, and Kirby Cane are all discussed in some detail in that volume. The Brooke Hall map is in the Norfolk Record Office: NRO T161D. The quotation from Roger North comes from his *Discourse of Fish and Fish Ponds* (London, 1712), page 21: see also C.K. Currie, 'Fishponds as Garden Features, 1550–1750', *Garden History* 18 (1990), 1, pages 22–46. Hamon le Strange's observations on dovecotes come from the draft of an unpublished pamphlet in the Norfolk Record Office: NRO le Strange ND 22.34. For the gardens at Stiffkey, see Hassell Smith in Taigel and Williamson (1991). For Oxnead, see Taigel and Williamson 1991, but for Nicholas Stone's sculptures see W.L. Spiers, *The Notebook of Nicholas Stone* (Walpole Society, Oxford, 1912). The Oxburgh map is in the National Trust archives. For the gardens at Raynham see Linda Campbell, 'Sir Roger Townshend and his Family'. For recent work on late medieval designed landscapes in England see Paul Everson, 'Bodiam Castle, East Sussex: a Fourteenth-Century Designed Landscape', in D. Morgan Evans, P. Salway and D. Thackray (eds), *'The Remains of Distant Times': Archaeology and the National Trust* (London, 1996); and Christopher Taylor, Paul Everson and W. Wilson-North, 'Bodiam Castle, Sussex', *Medieval Archaeology* 34 (1991), pages 155–7. For deer parks see Oliver Rackham, *Trees and Woodland in the British Landscape* (London, 1976) and Rackham, *The History of the Countryside* (London, 1986). For the later development of deer parks in Norfolk see John Dye's excellent 'Change in the Norfolk Landscape: the Decline of the Deer Park' (unpublished MA dissertation, Centre of East Anglian Studies, University of East Anglia, 1990). For Hunstanton park see Cord Oestmann, *Lordship and Community: the Lestrange Family and the Village of Hunstanton, Norfolk in the First Half of the Sixteenth Century* (Centre of East Anglian Studies/Boydell and Brewer 1994). The Hedenham map is also in the NRO, currently uncatalogued.

CHAPTER 2: THE LATE SEVENTEENTH AND EARLY EIGHTEENTH CENTURIES

For a general discussion of the development of architecture in this period, see Giles Worsley, *Classical Architecture in Britain: the Heroic Age* (New Haven, 1995); and for the role of 'gentlemen architects', R. Brown, *The Architectural Outsiders* (London, 1985). Garden design is dealt with by Tom Turner, *English Garden Design: Landscape and Styles Since 1660* (Woodbridge, 1985).

For Roger North and the building of Rougham Hall, see: H. Colvin and J. Newman, *Of Building: Roger North's Writings on Architecture* (Oxford, 1981); Tom Williamson, 'Roger North at Rougham: a Lost House and its Landscape', in C. Rawcliffe, R. Virgoe, and R. Wilson (eds), *Counties and Communities: Essays on East Anglian History Presented to Hassell Smith* (Norwich, 1996), pages 275–90.

Roger Pratt and the building of Ryston are dealt with in R.T. Gunther, *The Architecture of Sir Roger Pratt* (Oxford, 1928), and N. Silcox-Crowe, 'Roger Pratt 1620–1685: The Ingenious Gentleman Architect', in R. Brown, *The Architectural Outsiders* (London, 1985). For Pratt's account book see Norfolk Record Office Mf/Ro 219/1.

For Melton Constable, see Leonard Knyff and Johannes Kip, *Britannia Illustrata* (London, 1707); Christopher Hussey, 'Melton Constable', *Country Life* 64 (1928), pages 364–70, 402–9. For Roger North's acerbic comments on Jacob Astley and his building projects, see Colvin and Newman, *Of Building: Roger North's Writings*, page 9, and for his attack on Samuel Vincent, pages 7 and 72. The Buckenham Tofts map is in the Norfolk Record Office: Petre Box 8.

The history of the Fountaines and the building of Narford Hall are neatly summarised in J. Chambers, *General History of the County of Norfolk* (1829), pages 637–43. Haveringland Hall is shown as a marginal elevation on a map of 1738: NRO Mf/Ro 37/3.

For the development of 'late geometric' gardens in Norfolk see Taigel and Williamson, 'Some Early Geometric Gardens'. For the landscape at Rougham see Williamson, *Roger North at Rougham*; A. Davison, 'Rougham, the Documentary Evidence', in Alan Davison (ed.), 'Six Deserted Villages in Norfolk', *East Anglian Archaeology* 44 (1988); and A. Jessop (ed.), *The Autobiography of the Hon Roger North* (London, 1887). The information about the Raynham gardens is in the Raynham Hall archives; Edmund Prideaux's sketches of Raynham and Narford are in a private collection but photographic copies are kept at the National Monuments Record, Swindon, negative numbers BB90/1249 and AA75/2219.

CHAPTER 3: THE PALLADIAN AGE, c. 1720–50

For Palladianism and its political significance see Dan Cruikshank's excellent *Guide to the Georgian Buildings of Britain and Ireland* (London, 1985).

For Kimberley Hall, see A.M.F. Pickard, 'An Eighteenth-Century Building Campaign: the improvements at Kimberley Hall, 1755–58' (unpublished MA dissertation, Centre of East Anglian Studies, University of East Anglia, 1997).

For the building of Houghton Hall see Revd J.H. Broome, *Houghton and the Walpoles* (London and King's Lynn, 1865); J. Cornforth, 'Houghton: the Growth of an Idea', *Country Life*, (14 May 1987), pages 162–8; and J. Harris, 'The Architecture of the House', in A. Moore (ed.), *Houghton Hall: The Prime Minister, the Empress, and the Heritage* (London, 1996), pages 20–4.

The quotations concerning the size and construction of Houghton are from Sir John Clerke of Penicuik's journal of a tour in 1733 in the Scottish Record Office: SRO GD/18/120/7. The quotations from Lord Oxford, and from Sir Thomas Robinson, can be found in the Historic Manuscripts Commission's *Fifteenth Report, Appendix, Part VI: The Manuscripts of the Earl of Carlisle Preserved at Castle Howard* (London, 1907); that from Lord Hervey comes from the Earl of Ilchester, *Lord Hervey and His Friends* (London, 1952). The reference to the construction of Houghton 'Newtown' is from S. Markham, *John Loveday of Caversham, 1711–1789: the Life and Times of an Eighteenth-Century Onlooker* (London, 1984).

The best accounts of the building of Holkham Hall are: Leo Schmidt, 'Holkham Hall, Norfolk', *Country Life* (January 1980), pages 214–17, 298–301; C.M. Sicca, 'Holkham Hall', in B. Ford (ed.), *The Cambridge Guide to the Arts in Britain Volume 5: The Augustan Age* (Cambridge, 1991).

Langley and Gunton are discussed in O. Brackett, 'Langley Park, Norfolk', *Country Life* 62 (1927), pages 16–22; and G. Carter, *Gunton Park 1670–1987* (Norwich, 1988). For the evidence for the building of the hall in the 1730s, before Brettingham's involvement, see Norfolk Record Office BEA 9/7 433 X 5. The painting of George Proctor and friends hangs in the Castle Museum, Norwich.

The building of Wolterton Hall is described at length in Beverley Peter's masterful, but unfortunately unpublished MA dissertation, 'The Development of Wolterton Hall' (Centre of East Anglian Studies, University of East Anglia, 1991). The quotation from Thomas Ripley is from the Norfolk Record Office, WAL 1429.

For the development of the Houghton landscape, see: Tom Williamson, 'The Planting of the Park', in A. Moore (ed.), *Houghton Hall*, pages 41–7. See also David Yaxley, 'Houghton', in Alan Davison (ed.), 'Six Deserted Villages in Norfolk', *East Anglian Archaeology* 44 (1988), pages 83–94. Colen Campbell's plan of Houghton is published in his *Vitruvius Britannicus*, Vol. III (London, 1725) (although the plan itself was drawn up in 1722). Isaac Ware's plan of Bridgeman's new design for the park is published in his *The Plans, Elevations, and Sections; Chimney-pieces and Ceilings of Houghton in Norfolk* (London, 1735). For the best discussion of Bridgeman and his style see P. Willis, *Charles Bridgeman* (London, 1977). For the transformation of Houghton church, see David Yaxley. 'The Tower of Houghton St Martin Church', *The Annual Bulletin of the Norfolk Archaeological and Historical Research Group* 3 (1994), pages 46–50; and G. and A. Fenner, 'Houghton: the Church', in Davison (ed.) 'Six Deserted Villages in Norfolk', *East Anglian Archaeology* 44 (1988), pages 95–9. The Water House is dealt with by R. Bowden-Smith in *The Water House, Houghton Hall* (Woodbridge, 1987). The most important documentary evidence is in the Cambridge University Library, Cholmondeley Mss, 23/3; and in the archives at Houghton Hall, especially maps 1, 2, 23, 27 and 28; and documents A55, M24, and Box 1.

The discussion of the development of Holkham park is based on the following documents in the archives at the hall: A/10, A/11, A/32, A/33, A/34, A/35, A/36, A/37; and maps 2/1, 2/2, and 2/3. See also Susanna Wade Martins, *Holkham Park: Its Development Through Three Centuries* (Norwich, 1983); and Williamson, *Archaeology of the Landscape Park*.

The development of the Wolterton landscape is well documented in the archives at the hall and in the Norfolk Record Office. In the latter, see in particular WAL 1441/8 and 1429; in the former, Wolt 8/9, 8/13, 8/18, 8/20, 8/21, 8/29, 9/60, 10/20 and 10/99. See also Peters, *Wolterton*; and Williamson, *Archaeology of the Landscape Park*.

CHAPTER 4: AGE OF ELEGANCE: LATER GEORGIAN AND REGENCY

For a general discussion of country house architecture in the later eighteenth century see the later sections of Worsley, *Classical Architecture in Britain*, and Cruikshank, *Georgian Buildings*. For Norfolk, Nigel Wright, 'The Gentry and their Houses in Norfolk and Suffolk *c.* 1550–1850' (unpublished PhD thesis, Centre of East Anglian Studies, University of East Anglia, 1991). The best discussion of eighteenth-century gardening is in David Jacques, *Georgian Gardens: the Reign of Nature* (London, 1983); although for a slightly different view see Tom Williamson, *Polite Landscapes: Gardens and Society in Eighteenth-Century England* (London, 1995). For Capability Brown and his style see Dorothy Stroud, *Capability Brown* (London, 1957) and Roger Turner, *Capability Brown and the Eighteenth-Century English Landscape* (London, 1986).

For the social and economic background see Mark Girouard, *Life in the English Country House*; Paul Langford, *A Polite and Commercial People* (London, 1992); and N. MacKendrick, J. Brewer and J.H. Plumb, *The Birth of a Consumer Society* (London, 1982).

The architect John Soane is discussed by Dorothy Stroud, *The Architecture of Sir John Soane* (London, 1961). For Repton's activities as an architect see George Carter, 'Architecture', in George Carter, Patrick Goode and Kedrum Laurie, *Humphry Repton: Landscape Gardener* (Norwich, 1982). Samuel Driver's plan for Hillington is in the Norfolk Record Office: NRS 21369 Ffolkes.

The development of Holkham Park is once again well documented in the estate archives, in particular in John Sandys's planting book (uncatalogued); and in the following account books: A/Au/41; A/Au/50; A/45, A/46, A/47. Repton's Red Book for Holkham is also in the estate archives. For Coke's activities as an agricultural improver see N. Riches, *The Agricultural Revolution in Norfolk* (North Carolina, 1967); R.A.C. Parker, *Coke of Norfolk* (London, 1975); Susanna Wade Martins, *A Great Estate at Work* (Cambridge, 1980); and Williamson, *Archaeology of the Landscape Park*.

For information about the Earsham gardens see Norfolk Record Office: MEA 3/14–18; MEA 3/632; MEA 3/653; MEA 3/72–82. The quotations from William Windham's journal can be found in H. Baring (ed.), *The Diary of the Right Honourable William Windham 1784–1810* (London, 1868). For the information about parkland forestry see William Marshall, *The Rural Economy of Norfolk* (2 volumes, London, 1787), Vol. 1, pages 120–1; and Nathaniel Kent, *General View of the Agriculture of the County of Norfolk* (London, 1796), page 87.

The earthworks at Anmer are discussed in detail in B. Cushion, 'An Earthwork Survey of Anmer, Norfolk', *Medieval Settlement Research Group Annual Report* 9 (1994), pages 27–9. For a general discussion of earthwork features in landscape parks see T. Williamson, *Archaeology of the Landscape Park*. For more general discussion of settlement desertion caused by emparking see Chris Taylor, *Village and Farmstead* (London, 1988).

Heacham is dealt with in R. Wilson and A. Mackley, 'Founding a Landed Dynasty, Building a Country House: the Rolfes of Heacham in the Eighteenth Century', in Rawcliffe, Virgoe, and Wilson (eds), *Counties and Communities*, pages 307–28: Rolfe's account of the building and landscaping work can be found in the Norfolk Record Office, HEA 488 and 489. The building and alteration of Honing Hall is dealt with by Nigel Wright, *Norfolk Gentry and their Houses*. Beeston is discussed by R. Haslam, 'Beeston Hall', *Country Life* 172 (1983), pages 270–4: see also the account books in Norfolk Record Office, MC36/136. The quotation from James Grigor comes from *Eastern Arboretum*. For the development of country house visiting see Adrian Tinniswood, *A History of Country House Visiting* (London, 1989).

Repton's career has recently been examined in detail by Stephen Daniels, *Humphry Repton: landscape gardening and the geography of Georgian England* (New Haven, 1999): see also Dorothy Stroud, *Humphry Repton* (London, 1962). For the ideological implications of Repton's later landscape style see S. Daniels 'The Political Landscape', in Carter, Goode, and Laurie (eds), *Humphry Repton*, pages 110–21. Most of the text of the Sheringham Red Book can be found in John Claudius Loudon, *The Landscape Gardening and Landscape Architecture of the Late Humphry Repton Esq.* (London, 1840). Further information about Sheringham can be found in Susan Yaxley (ed.), *Sheringhamia: The Journal of Abbot Upcher 1813–1816* (Stibbard, 1986).

CHAPTER 5: THE NINETEENTH CENTURY

For the development of country houses in the nineteenth century see Mark Girouard, *The Victorian Country House* (London, 1979) and Jill Franklin, 'The Victorian Country House', in G.E. Mingay (ed.), *The Rural Idyll* (London, 1989). The career of W.J. Donthorne is discussed by Roderick O'Donell, 'W.J. Donthorne', *Architectural History* 21 (1978), pages 83–92. The building of Shadwell Hall is discussed in Girouard, *Country Life* 136 (1964), pages 98–102. The description of Stow Bardolph is from *The Builder* (1873) pages 406–7.

The best general account of garden design in the nineteenth century is Brent Elliott, *Victorian Gardens* (London, 1986). For William Sawrey Gilpin see Sophie Piebenga, 'William Sawrey Gilpin (*c.* 1762–1843): Picturesque Improver', *Journal of Garden History* 22 (1994), pages 175–96. This account of his work at Wolterton is based on the following documents at Wolterton Hall: Wolt Box B; 10/100; 10/101; 10/102; 10/103. For William Andrews Nesfield, see Christopher Ridgway, 'William Andrews Nesfield: between Uvedale Price and Isambard Kingdom Brunel', *Journal of Garden History* 13, 1 and 2 (1993), pages 69–89.

The gardens at Lynford are described in the *Gardeners' Chronicle* (20 September 1884); those at Hillington in the *Gardeners' Chronicle* (1893), pages 771–2. The quotation about the gardens at Kimberley is from Grigor, *Eastern Arboretum*, pages 275–6. The building of Bylaugh Hall is described in *The Athenaeum* (February 1851); and in *The Builder* (1852), pages 518–19. Additional information is from the sales catalogue of 1917.

POSTSCRIPT

The decline of Norfolk's landed estates is discussed in P. Barnes, *Norfolk Landowners since 1880* (Norwich, 1993). The quotation about Felbrigg comes from R.W. Ketton-Cremer, *Felbrigg: the Story of a House* (London, 1982). See also C. Wakeling, *Change or Decay: the ways in which Norfolk houses have been adapted to new uses* (Norwich, 1976). The Acquisition Reports drawn up by the Forestry Commission are in the archives at Santon Downham, near Brandon, Suffolk.

INDEX

Figures in italics denote illustrations